FIRST 1000 DAYS OF STARTUP

DECODING FINANCE FOR ENTREPRENEURS

100 days   500 days   1000 days

SUNIL KUMAR PATHAK

FCA, ACS, LLB, IP, RV

notionpress.com

INDIA · SINGAPORE · MALAYSIA

Notion Press

No. 8, 3rd Cross Street
CIT Colony, Mylapore
Chennai, Tamil Nadu – 600004

First Published by Notion Press 2020
Copyright © Sunil Kumar Pathak 2020
All Rights Reserved.

ISBN 978-1-64899-998-7

Dedicated

☗☘

to

my father Shri. Jagdish Pathak
and mother Lt. Smt. Shanti Devi
for their inspiration
and
my friends, clients and readers
for sharing their experience and their
continued belief and support.

Contents

This is the only stage that is completely under your command, and So you do not need to rush but to get fully assured of the idea, facts, logic and corporate environment.

These are days to prove yourself as well as your business model and announce your commitments to the world. These are days of a rollercoaster ride, and your feelings—pathetic, joyful, suicidal and awesome—shall keep changing every passing moment. People will have their own views be it your friends or parents. Everybody will be concerned and shall make you concerned unless destiny has something else for you. But this also defines whether you are going to be a successful entrepreneur or end up with a golden experience of a failed start-up. It is the most important stage of your organization as the mess created at this stage cannot be cleaned by any future actions.

Section 2   The First 1000 Days   73

Now, as you have passed the test of time and are ready for the next league, so, in addition to supporting your finance department, which will perform its basic functions, you must continue to keep an eye on the bigger canvas.

Section 3 Beyond 1000 Days   177

Puneet Pushkarna Profile

Puneet Pushkarna is currently General Partner of Solmark, a Private Equity fund formed by a group of tech entrepreneurs who have launched and built several companies and bring expertise in all aspects of growing a company in a competitive global marketplace. Solmark's target portfolios include FinTech, Business Platforms, Cloud Technologies, Analytics, Data Management, MedTech and Customer Experience Management companies.

Prior to this, he was the President of Headstrong, a highly specialized deep-domain business in the Capital Markets that helped its customers through a strong process-centric digital technology services platform, leading to transformation in the front, middle and back office. Headstrong eventually got acquired by Genpact in 2011.

He was the co-founder of TechSpan, a Goldman Sachs backed design thinking and business solutions consulting organization, focused on e-business value chain management. Techspan consistently ranked amongst the fastest growing companies in Silicon Valley. He was part of the founding team that helped grow HCL America into what is now HCL Technologies.

He sits on a number of Boards/Advisory Boards including:

- Chairman of Servion Global Solutions Ltd, an end-to-end proactive Customer Experience Management firm
- Chairman of Innoveo, a Zurich based InsureTech company

- Senior Director, Everstone Capital, a Singapore based PE Fund
- Board of Governors, IIM Nagpur
- Industry Advisory Board of SP Jain School of Management
- Advisory Board of Ecosystm, a Digital Research Platform
- Member of SMART (Singapore **MIT** Alliance for Research & Technology) Innovation/Ignition Grant Advisory Board.
- Advisory Board of Evolko, a cloud based EMR and HealthRadar company
- Member Review Panel, Central Core Funding scheme run by the **NRF** (National Research Foundation) under the PMO in Singapore
- Judge, Innovators Under 35, a competition run by MIT Technology's EmTech Asia to identify 20 of the most promising innovators in Asia.

He is involved with a number of philanthropic initiatives and is the Patron of **IFA** (Indian Foundation for the Arts), and is on the Management Committee of **SIFAS** (Singapore Indian Fine Arts Society).

Puneet has been involved with **TiE** (The Indus Entrepreneurs), one of the largest Entrepreneur networks in the world. He currently is the Chairman Emeritus of TiE Singapore, and is also a member of the Board of Trustees for TiE Global, the apex management body for all the TiE Chapters in over 60 countries in the world.

Foreword

I am delighted to see that Sunil Pathak has written a very engaging and comprehensive account of the whole start-up process, based on his extensive personal experience and his engagement with the ecosystem from a complete 360 degree point of view. Sunil had a very interesting challenge in this book, and he has done an admirable job of it. Rather than write yet another academic or consulting text, he has written a book with concrete actionable steps. He has laid emphasis on the process and covered not only the broader contours of ideation to enterprise building, but has covered even the minutiae details from incorporation, financing, team building, etc.

I have been on both sides of the aisle; having been an entrepreneur and now an investor. As an investor, my main criteria to invest in a business is the team and the preparedness of the team to navigate the vagaries of the business. I think Sunil's ready reckoner is an exceptional guide to the whole journey. Having an idea and hoping for it to be successful is a hard crystal gazing exercise. However, being prepared for the changes that might come and hence PLANNING for it is the only way that you ensure that your chances of success improve. This book is a great guide to the preparedness and planning process.

I am sure the reader will learn a great deal from this book and for an aspiring entrepreneur, this will serve as a great compass to help her/him navigate the complex task of building and scaling a Start-up. I wish, this kind of book was available when I launched my first start-up.

My thanks to Sunil for putting pen to paper and showing the path to the budding entrepreneurs!

Puneet Pushkarna

Foreword

I am delighted to write the foreword for "First 1000 days of Start up".

My journey of launching Brainvisa and later on FirstCry taught me many Lessons of starting and scaling a business and we all keep learning with passing stages of business. Starting from the idea to unicorn stage, you come across immense number & quantum of hurdles which at times may be due to sheer ignorance or lack of knowledge about financial and legal aspects of running a business.

Getting funded by venture capitalists and PE funds comes at cost, which can be onerous at times. While such risk capital is usually good for company's growth and a strong validation of past performance but founder's have to be super careful of financial and legal implication of such negotiation and documentation. Having important basic business facts around in form of a book is great idea and this book fulfils that need.

Sunil Pathak, who is a friend and a learned professional, has been mentoring many start ups and doing management consulting to companies across the industry verticals. I recommended him to share his knowledge of start up eco-system with all the dreamers and entrepreneurs.

I am sure the whole gamut of the book shall prove to all your readers an important tool for their venture. Wish you all the very best !!

Supam Maheshwari
Co-Founder and CEO
FirstCry.com

Preface

The idea for this book, **The First 1000 Days of a Start-up,** came to my mind through my decade-old consulting journey with multiple business owners and other chief executives at the different stages of their life.

The solution to the same problem for different people and that too at different stages of their professional or personal life becomes very different. The competency, financial capabilities, age, risk appetite and wisdom play a direct role in making crucial decisions like launching a new business. We fully understand that one size does not fit all.

I have also noticed that people interpret financial statements and commercial facts very differently due to the lack of knowledge and ignorance of basic finance and its terminology. Moreover, when a budding entrepreneur conceives an idea and throws all his/her energy into manifesting that idea into action and starts taking care of core business needs, which ideally should be, finance takes the back seat. To me, that is the starting point of ignored financial affairs for an organization.

According to Darwin's theory of evolution, when wings, tails and limbs are not used wisely and appropriately, they vanish. Similarly, when the finance, which is the blood of an organization, bears the brunt of ignorance, it starts ignoring the organization too.

With this problem in mind and timely treatment of this problem, the idea of sharing my knowledge with all of you struck me. Therefore, I thought of making my experience and knowledge of business economics available to everyone without any face-time or consulting fees.

I got the idea of segmenting this book into three parts inspired by an old saying in Punjabi, *"Pehle sal chatti, pher hatti, pher khatti."* This means that in the first year, the business is non-profitable, in the second year it breaks-even, and in the third year, it makes a profit. Hence, it takes 1000 days to build a stable and profit-making enterprise. This ancient wisdom is prevalent in many cultures across India including Gujarati and Marwari.

As mentioned earlier, the book is divided into the following three parts:

- **Before You Start**
- **The First 1000 Days**
- **Beyond 1000 Days**

The above division suggests that you must plan your business meticulously, and then give it the appropriate time to settle, or even if it is settled, keep the focus until you become a unicorn or you learn to run a profit-making SME. If the journey of hardship continues beyond 1000 days, one should do some introspection and accept the failure gracefully if needed.

Berkshire Hathaway Vice Chairman Mr. Charlie Munger once said, *"The best thing a human being can do is help another human being know more."* In today's world, the strength of a nation is not measured by firepower but by its economic value and wealth. Be it a grand vision of building a five-trillion USD Indian economy or increasing the economic contribution of MSME from the existing 29% to 50% of India's GDP, the growth of MSME is the backbone and will play a pivot role in the times to come.

Before a proper finance department could be afforded and could function under the ownership of a successful entrepreneur, appropriate financial practices have to be adopted and applied by an entrepreneur to maintain stability in business.

The primary objective of this book is to educate people about complete life cycle of business and create financial awareness. This book may not be a solution to all your financial problems or it may not teach you technical intricacies of financial management, but it will definitely provoke you to think in the right direction, resulting in taking the right decision at the right time.

The other objective of this book is to show how financial theories and economic wisdom could be applied to solve real-life problems. I have made a sincere attempt to relate the theories to practice.

Congratulation on your investment in this book, and let me assure you that you will not regret it. There could be many books in the market on start-ups and all could be valuable, but the complex language and use of technical jargon can make those books boring at times. I have tried to maintain a simple, conversational style throughout the book just like what I could have suggested in a face-to-face meeting. I have invested a substantial part of my career as a corporate advisor, management consultant, growth advisor, mentor, investor and entrepreneur, so this book is more about sharing my experiences with you all. After completing this book, you will know the following aspects of business:

- Why and how to start your own business?
- Plan before you leave your present engagement to commence a business
- The concept of financial management, few widely used financial principles and its importance to small businesses
- Few financial management practices and rules that are commonly applicable to small businesses
- The basics of making a pitch presentation

- Understanding start-up funding and tools to approach investors and fund houses

- The basic idea of the valuation of your company and the legal terms used by investors

- Various internal controls and check systems for a start-up and growing business

- The basics of working capital management

- The basics of corporate finance and tools of finance

- How to make the best use of your consultant and advisors

We are lucky to be a part of the most sophisticated and fabulous generation and with utmost care and intelligence, we can create an impact on the whole world through our ideas and generate wealth for our nation. Your business is not only a physical manifestation of your idea and dreams but also a contribution to nation-building. Wish you best of luck.

Thank you!

Acknowledgement

Book writing takes lots of studies and calls for brainstorming, intellectual discussions, professional help, guidance and encouragement. I have drawn upon vast amounts of financial literature, articles, blogs and research reports from many people and institutions. I naturally owe to them. Therefore, my intellectual capital in the form of this book belongs to all those contributors.

I have also benefited immensely from the insights and experiences of my co-workers and professional friends with whom I had multiple rounds of discussions.

I want to express my heartiest gratitude for the contribution done by my friends, Mr. Rahul Kishore and Mr. Manav Mehra for sharing their insights and experiences. I also wish to thank Ms. Garvita for her graphic and visual art contributions. I also had the privilege of getting help & guidance from Mr. Shivjit Kullar, Mr. Sauraj Bhardwaj, Mr. Anant Verma, Mr. Vipin Sharma, Mr. Puneet Sharma, Mr. Ranjit Raina Mrs. Neena Sen, Mr. Rishabh Pathak among others.

I want to express my deep gratitude, of course, to my wife, Archna and my children Shreemayi and Shashwat for their sacrifice of family time and constant encouragement for completing the publication of book.

Covid-19
New Normal, New Dawn

In history, never before the world has faced a worldwide lockdown that deprived millions of people of their livelihoods and for some even their lives. The situation has once again challenged *homo sapiens'* survival instincts, intellectual prowess and strategy to remain the most powerful being on the planet.

The coronavirus outbreak, which was first detected in China, has infected people around the world. Its spread has left businesses around the world counting the costs and damages.

The pandemic has pushed the global economy into a recession, a state in which the economy shrinks and growth stops. The International Monetary Fund (IMF) estimated that the global economy will be growing at -3% in 2020, which is an outcome "far worse" than the 2009 global financial crises. This year, economies such as the US, Japan, and the UK are expected to contract by 5.9%, 5.2% and 6.5% respectively.

According to an assessment by the World Economic Forum (WEF), supporting SMEs and large businesses is crucial for maintaining employment and financial stability. As documented in April 2020 Global Financial Stability Report, capital flows to emerging markets are rapidly receding, while global risk aversion has spiked.

As investors fear that the spread of the coronavirus will destroy economic growth and the government's actions may not be enough to stop the decline and erosion of wealth, the stock market all over the world has declined substantially. Oil prices around the globe have receded to 21 years low and the US oil prices went even negative for the first time.

The COVID-19 pandemic is impacting emerging markets like India through an unprecedented mix of domestic and external shocks, the combined effects of which are hard to predict. Among these, emerging markets are confronting a sharp tightening in global financial conditions and stricter norms of financing for start-ups.

According to the Organization for Economic Co-operation and Development (OECD), for every month of lockdown, there will be a loss of 2% in the annual growth of the GDP of a country.

So while the pandemic will affect all businesses because manpower itself shall be a scarce resource due to social distancing norms, businesses in hospitality, tourism, entertainment, aviation and logistics, etc. are prone to bigger damages. The income of people at large will be affected, which shall consequently affect the purchasing power and so the demand for commodities is bound to go down. This will necessarily entail sharp economic slowdowns, starting from closures of workplaces and factories of non-essential goods to behavioural changes in consumption patterns at large.

The COVID-19 pandemic is proving to be a challenge for many of us, and it shall change the way we behave and perceive things. Many of our habits shall change. This unexpected and adverse shift in habits and mindset has already impacted the economies heavily. But in some cases, this situation has shaped a new line of opportunities. Adaptability and creative decision-making will play a key role in the sustainability of enterprises.

I believe that just like SARS 2003 changed our outlook on e-commerce, the COVID-19 too will pave way for adopting a new outlook on industries and innovative product lines like facial recognition and blockchains.

Ideas and technologies that have a proportional relationship with new norms of society and consumer behaviour will evolve rapidly as a result of mass confinement, safety concerns and inventory shortages.

To my mind, industries that look appealing for the post-COVID new normal are as follows:

1. Smartphones commerce and no-touch alternate digital payment options

2. CRM software application and digital framework for back-end management

3. Opportunities around automation and chatbots, etc.

4. Premium services of faster home delivery

5. Rich content media streaming applications

6. Digital and virtual experiential marketing

7. Virtual and online medical consulting and medicine delivery

8. Hygiene maintenance services around home and workplaces

9. Self-care and fitness industry

10. Online and interactive education platforms

11. Virtual meetings and conference applications

12. IoT (Internet of things) to IoE (Internet of everything) applications. Consumers will prefer SMART of everything, TV to refrigerator and light to a car

13. Mobile communication, satellite tracking and internet speed (5G and faster research on maybe 6G/7G)

14. Artificial intelligence, machine learning, big data analytics and robotics shall redefine the technology space

15. Insurance and simplification of buying an insurance policy. I see a good adaptation of technology in the insurance sector.

Mr. Ratan Tata, one of the most influential business magnates in India and also my inspiration, believes, "Entrepreneurs in India can find answers to how to operate in the post-COVID world. It is an opportunity for an entrepreneur to shine and new ideas to thrive even in the face of this hardship."

According to a billionaire entrepreneur Mark Cuban, India could potentially lead the change in the post-COVID world with its vast array of engineers and investment opportunities.

India is a goldmine for the success of any business for the following reasons and these reasons shall continue to be there in the post-COVID-19 era too:

1. It has the second-largest population in the world growing at a rate of approximately 1%.

2. More than 50% of its population is below the age of 25 and more than 65% below the age of 35. It is expected that, in 2020, the average age of an Indian will be 29 years.

3. The country has the cheapest data rates globally and a high growth rate of internet penetration.

4. The country has the second-largest smartphone population in the world. Roughly 600 million monthly active customers access the World Wide Web.

5. There is improving institutional and government support and corporate participation.

6. The literacy rate is more than 75% and there are a large number of English-speaking working populations.

7. The size of the Indian economy is substantial. In addition, the country has an above-average GDP growth rate and a good amount of international trade.

Around the world, many countries have been announcing relief packages in the form of liquidity and ease of doing business and compliances. In India, the government has announced the program called Atmanirbhar Bharat Abhiyan to encourage medium, small and micro enterprises (MSMEs) to build a self-reliant economy. As per the forecast by many international institutions, India's GDP growth rate shall touch zero. But I believe that being an agriculture-based economy and along with other positive factors of the country, the Indian economy shall bounce back with double strength in very less revival time.

However, a few questions shall remain open as to how do we reduce our national import bills, how to re-engage the migrant labourers and how to be the innovation capital of the world. We do have market, manpower and mind and maybe money is the fourth pillar that can help revive our economy. The government of India has taken few steps considering the budgetary constraint the country faces, and I am sure that in the long run these limited liquidity measures, without much affecting the fiscal deficit of the country, will prove to be a pragmatic and balanced approach.

The government has also redefined the meaning of MSME and now both the manufacturing and service sectors are on the same qualifying matrix. Companies with an investment of less than Rs. 1 crore and turnover under Rs. 5 crores will fall under the category of micro-units, while small businesses will be categorized based on investment less than Rs. 10 crores and turnover under Rs. 50 crores. Medium enterprises will be defined based on investment under Rs. 20 crores and turnover less than Rs. 100 crores. The basic purpose of such a change is to cover a large number of organizations.

Now, I am going to list a few such important stimuli which can be helpful if you are facing a financial crunch. Though many of these schemes have cut-off dates and I am not sure how relevant this maybe when you read it, I am sure these stimuli shall be there in some other shape or form and you must try to dig deeper and collect information in this regard.

Start-up India schemes (Covid-19)

There are many schemes for funding, marketing support and grants available both in debt and equity mode. You may also look at all compliance relaxations, mentoring avenues and other incubation facilities. You may visit and keep a tab on www.startupindia.gov.in for more details as this site keeps on updating the useful information in the MSME ecosystem in line with government announcements.

Covid-19 emergency credit line (CECL)

The government-owned lender SBI has offered a maximum loan amount of up to Rs. 200 crores or 10% of the existing fund-based working capital limits that can be availed under this emergency line. The facility will be available till the end of June 2020, and it specifically aims at MSME borrowers. These loans will be given at a flat rate of 7.25%. In addition, SBI has also been doing relaxed calculations on working capital needs by accepting higher collection days.

Rs. 3 lakh crores collateral-free loan

Banks and NBFCs will offer up to 20% of the entire outstanding credit as of February 29, 2020, to MSMEs. Units with up to Rs. 25 crores outstanding credit and Rs. 100 crores turnover are eligible for taking these loans. These loans will have four-year tenure with a moratorium of 12 months on the principal payment. The scheme can be availed till October 31, 2020. The government will provide a complete credit guarantee cover to lenders.

Rs. 20,000 crores subordinate debt

MSMEs that have been declared NPAs or stressed ones will be eligible for equity support as the government will facilitate Rs. 20,000 crores as subordinate debt. The government will also provide Rs. 4,000 crores to CGTMSE that will offer partial credit guarantee support to banks for lending to MSMEs.

Rs. 50,000 crores fund of funds

There is a provision to create a fund of funds, and eligible MSME shall get equity infusion through this scheme so that their capacities could be enhanced.

Global tenders scheme amended

To remove the unfair competition from foreign companies in terms of government procurement tenders due to the size and strength, the government has announced that it will not allow global tenders in such schemes up to Rs. 200 crores.

Clearing MSME dues

The government and central public sector enterprises will release all pending MSME payments in 45 days. Also, more and more FinTech enterprises will be used to boost transaction-based lending using data by the e-marketplace. The facilities of invoice factoring and bill discounting have also been implemented through public-private partnerships for the MSME sector.

These Covid-19 related schemes, in addition to facilities, are available from banks and other institutions and more importantly from SIDBI, which also offers various types of soft loans as well as equity funding products.

I sincerely believe that you will take benefit of all possible schemes, and through your fine sense of wisdom on expense management and creative intelligence, we all will see the new dawn, and the light of success shall prevail everywhere.

Section 1

BEFORE YOU
START YOUR BUSINESS

Chapter 1.1

Your Present Financial Status

Before you start dreaming of a new business idea and its commencement, the most important thing you have to ensure is your preparedness on the personal front. If you are not doing great at present and the business idea is coming out of any frustration, then it is time to  introspect and not escape. Your business should come out of your choice and not compulsion.

Your preparedness depends on the present stage of your life. I am categorizing the checkpoints for various age groups of dreamers.

Youngblood (up till 30 years)

You are blessed with fewer liabilities unless there are specific circumstances and some special exigencies. I trust that you are at the beginning of your career and you have yet not seen the practical business life. It is a good time to dream big without much trail of on-going liabilities, but I must warn you that this is also the golden time of your life as far as the energy level of your body and mind is concerned. You should not waste it without giving it a deeper thought or without consulting your parents, spouse and guardians for their support and motivation. Please check the following:

1. The financial position of your parents as to their dependence on you or their expectations in terms of your financial contribution in running the family. If you need to contribute essentially then think this through more granularly.

2. Are you and your dependent family members covered well with medical emergency funds and/or a medical insurance policy? If yes, then good, else get a family floater policy from a good insurance company.

3. Do you aspire for higher education? If yes, think about your business decision once more. Once you start your business and money starts flowing into your life, education takes a back seat, and in many cases, the dream of getting a qualification remains unfulfilled.

4. Have you taken a higher education loan? If yes, please take stock of your liability commencement date as you cannot just shift the EMI obligation to your parents' or spouse's shoulders.

5. Are you already in some job or have you signed any kind of employment agreement or even internship with a clause that restricts you from doing business full-time or part-time? If yes, consult a lawyer friend or just go and talk to your employer and take written permission for exploring this new idea.

Mature executives (beyond 30)

This age group, depending upon the education and stage of career, is more likely to have a good amount of ongoing liabilities of the family, be it in terms of their parents or children.

You may or may not be supported by the earnings of your spouse. It is important to note that what is being discussed here is a mid-aged person who is the single earning member of the family. This person has an average performing job and has liabilities like home loans, car loans, medical insurance, children's education, parents' well-being and lots of other accountabilities.

I would not say that you are ineligible to dream about owning a business, but the circumstances should be made such that you could handle the peaks and trough of business at least for the first three years without affecting your own financial position.

The preparation time of approximately a year should include the following:

- Ideating and preserving to see the result—take one step ahead or even back maybe. Test it beyond doubt.
- Do a live simulation of your business
- Note the response and reaction of people
- Zero your liabilities or reduce to the extent possible
- Talk to your family and convince them. You yourself should plan to pay for your failure and not your family.
- Save some capital and emergency fund

Before you take the plunge, please check the following:

1. Make a worksheet of your income and expenditures and look at the savings you have done till now. You may also include your spouse's earnings if any. Your savings and the residual income after you commence your business must finance the routine expenses at least for a year.

2. Check whether you have relevant insurances like a family floater medical policy for yourself and all the dependent family members. You must have this for your family because if they are in bad shape, you will never be able to give 100% of your energy to your business.

3. Make sure to have a term policy for your life depending on the income and expenses and net worth situation. Ideally, you should also have an accident policy and critical illness coverage that will secure you against the disabilities and discontinuance of your work and its spilling effect on your family and business.

4. You may be in employment, and here you must check your employment letter for non-conflict and non-compete clauses and extended legal time coverage (in general it is from six months to one year). If it is so, then make sure to take the written consent of your employer. These are the precautions that must be taken when your proposed business idea falls in the category of competing or conflicting business as compared to the business of your employer.

5. Check your aptitude for being an entrepreneur, and it is simple to do that. Just ask yourself the following questions:

   a. Are you ready for the uncertainty of income and risk of losing your own hard-earned money in sustaining yourself and your business?

   b. Are you ready for long hours of work and does your health allow that? You are going to have less quality of life at least for some time.

   c. Are you ready to accept the complaints, discouragements and failures? You need to own the success and failure. You may like to share your success with your co-founder or key stakeholders/employees but your failures shall be solely yours.

   d. Do you love to do what you are contemplating doing? Remember, a business is like a baby that you are trying to give birth to, and once it is born, you need to love it passionately and unconditionally. You do not need to be stubborn, but the conceptual mania to become a successful entrepreneur tends to prevail.

e. Do you know the end stage of your proposed business? We hear a lot about the first-mover advantage, but knowing the end game is even more important. If there is no first-mover advantage, it may be better at times because whatever you ideate shall be free of all the shortcomings of previous ventures, and you can always improve upon the goodness of your idea. If you know the end stage of your business, then it is easier to not only become sustainable but also rack the highest profit in the long run because you do not need to develop a market for your product and services.

Chapter 1.2

How Much Capital You Have

You can travel till the fuel lasts or you get towed. This very well applies to business as money is the fuel to run business and if you exhaust this resource then either you stop or you need external support to keep moving.

From day one and probably till the prototype stage, nobody is going to trust you and fund you except yourself and maybe the co-founder or your immediate family.

So before you announce, you must count the money you have to reach a certain stage at which you can ask for little help from your friends and family. This may not be an intelligent investment for them, but depending upon the trust and affection they might have for you, they will support you financially or otherwise. You should not try to sell the business idea but just ask for their belief in you.

Here are some factors that you should keep in mind while counting any money as your capital:

- The bank balance which is surplus should only be considered after taking out your committed expenses

- Available cash, foreign exchange or gold (except jewellery) be considered

- Fixed deposit and recurring deposits can be included

- Do not count anything which is receivable from friends and family. In other words, do not include the money that you lent to your friends and family until you receive the same.

- Do not count any incentive that is expected from your present employer as the same may not be paid to you if you leave them or they get to know about your plan

- You should not count any equity stock you have that is trading high unless you book the profit by selling it immediately.

- You should not count any investment that is subject to lock-in or exit load.

- You should not count any real estate that cannot be sold at your disposal because when you need money, the same may not be available for your rescue due to various market conditions.

- You may count the mutual fund investment you have unless there are lock-ins and exit loads, etc. In general, if you have invested mindfully, these are open-ended and shall not have exit loads.

Also, at this stage, you must decide the risk appetite for yourself and maybe you should designate certain funds as 'capital at risk' from your side and limit your loss at that stage. Once you have this demarcated fund for your start-up, it acts as a great affirmation of the fact that "you have enough money to set up primary pillars of business and touch the revenue stage".

You don't always need enormous capital if you start right and act as per your plan. The way to succeed in business is to have a focused mind and do one thing really well, which becomes the differentiator. To ensure longer sustainability of your small risk capital, adopt the following disciplines from day one:

- Think twice before you spend even a single penny and find out cheaper alternatives and rule them out before committing the expenses

- Do small things and take up small assignments to facilitate your bigger vision

- Keep earning through the best skills that you have acquired till date

- Always try to rent out than buying unless it makes an absolute sense

- Try to pay in terms of equity rather than cash as this is how you can make a good team too

- Leverage your existing assets like electronic equipment, home/office space, vehicle, friend circle, society, etc.

In the end, if you have invested all and there is no hope for getting the fund in the next 30 days, you might like to gracefully accept and keep the business idea burning inside you and start doing something

which gives you immediate money. Here, you must be ready to run the idea on the back-burner as a part-time activity till you get funds to grow it further. To buy some more time or to bridge the cash flow gap, you may also look for a like-minded partner with a solid financial background, who can help you sustain the business for some more time. However, having a co-founder on board has its own merits and demerits, which we will cover in detail later.

Have the courage to be at the edge, but do not be a fool to fall.

Chapter 1.3

Your Business Idea

All of us keep getting ideas to get rid of our boss, and we all know that the excitement of building a new business from scratch is much greater than the fear of failure. One of the factors for which the number of failures in the start-up ecosystem is high is the fact that there was no audience for the product or services in the real marketplace.

The basic framework for finalizing a viable and sustainable idea is to ask the first three important questions namely, "WHY" followed by "HOW" and "WHAT".

These three questions construct the basic testing template for your business idea. Earning money and becoming successful is not the answer to WHY but it is an outcome of why and what you do in a certain manner and process.

Knowing your WHY is not only the way to get success but also to be doubly assured that this is the only way for sustainable and stable growth.

HOW is always based on your skill sets and propriety process, and this is what makes you unique as this is where you put in a value proposition for your target customers.

Knowing WHAT is the simplest as all the companies around the globe understand the product or services they offer. You could choose *carrot or stick* here, and by this phrase I mean either you can manipulate your consumer-base and do a price competition or simply motivate them to use your product or services.

A good business intelligence report must answer the above three questions to an extent that it further answers various micro questions about the operational plan, leadership, quality assurance and financial management.

It is extremely necessary to do detailed business research on the product and services along with the research on the target market and geography.

Good business research will help you in identifying the measures required for success of business idea, knowing any potholes and remedies thereof.

You must ask yourself the following questions before doing the research:

- What problem does my product or service solve?
- Who is the target audience for my product or service?
- Which geography and population strata the product or service fits the most?
- Where will they buy it? For example, specialty shops, department stores, online, mobile app, or home delivery.
- What can be a smart price for the product?
- What will be my nearest competing product or service?

The more narrowly you could define your business and your target market, the better it is. So, you must create a niche for yourself in the marketplace as it is the key to success for even the biggest companies.

Once you are ready with the final product or service, which can fly in the marketplace, do the following:

1. Map the global economy and conduct country-specific business research

2. Conduct industry research and research on any legal issue which may arise

3. Do competitor analysis and try to find out the strength and weakness

4. Check all the failures in this industry (to the extent you can) and make it a point not to repeat the same mistakes in your business

5. Analyze the endgame of this industry and how it will finally culminate

6. Plan your stages and growth charts along with action points

A good idea, implemented in an appropriate manner and timely fashion, is bound to succeed.

In short, you must be absolutely clear as to why you want to start your business and after that create a robust process discipline for consistent quality and finally keep innovating around your deliverables with the passage of time.

Chapter 1.4

Market Research

It is better to fail a hundred times on paper than failing once on the ground. Failure breaks you and hits your self-confidence and financial competency big time.

Now, after the business research is done and you are sure about the success of the product in the marketplace, it is time for a reality check. Communicate your idea with friends and family and see the first reaction. Note their reaction as initial feedback and improvise, and without mentioning it, convince them in one or more meetings to use your product or even join your business as partners. This is like homework with no real consequences.

You may need to conduct formal product and market research without investing much money, and in this case, you can hire a few freelancers with the pre-set questionnaire for the relevant audience. It is important to conduct market research in appropriate places or areas to get in touch with the real target audience. For example, you cannot go to a golf club to research a product that is meant for the lower-middle-income group.

Big Bazar and la marche, both are departmental stores, but they have different niches; Big Bazar caters to bargain-minded shoppers, while la-marche appeals to upscale, quality-conscious customers.

Many new business ideas and offerings are successful today because their promoters identified the problem of the society or an unmet demand and verified the feasibility of contemplated solutions. You cannot afford to waste your time, money and other resources in producing something that is not saleable.

The best medium to authenticate your feelings about your business idea and the result of your business research is to

- check online what people are looking for
- ask the potential customer their views about doing business in this segment
- use the product or service first to identify what all can be improved
- meet any incubator firm to understand the recent trends
- meet any of the proposed suppliers of input for your business
- go to a potential customer and show them the sample or prototype (if have one) and ask them if they would like to buy it
- visit a few exhibitions and see the market response/macro data based on the category of your offerings

The above exercise shall give you more insight into the real marketplace and help you to be firm and assertive in presenting your business proposition to stakeholders in near future.

You must also keep tweaking your plan as per the market research rather than sticking to the original idea as this will help to enhance the adaptability and success of your products.

After conducting market research, you should get clarity on the following aspects:

1. Estimated demand for your product or service

2. Type and size of the existing market and competition

3. Effective marketing and distribution channels

4. What can be your USP (unique selling proposition)

5. Convenient Product prices for the customers

6. What government regulation you may have to follow

7. Macro data of industry for analytics

Once you have done your research about the demand, price sensitivity and business feasibility, you must document these findings as these will prove to be valuable data points when you approach a professional investor any time in the lifecycle of your company.

Chapter 1.5

Business Plan Sketch

Business planning is a science of creating a business, and it requires some advanced skills related to finance such as sales estimation, scenario simulation, trend analysis and many other forecasts. But at this stage, you must make a rough sketch to understand the basic viability, which implies the following aspects:

1. Decide the budget for capital expenditure like buying computers or software depending upon the need of the business

2. Decide the manpower required to run the business at a basic level. The manpower cost must be correlated with the level of revenue and their optimum productivity.

3. Decide your role and that of the co-founder if any, and decide the macro distribution of accountability

4. Decide the place of work and rental expenses if any. Here, you must decide whether the business, depending on its nature, can be done from home or a residential area or you need a corporate office. Co-working spaces too could be considered depending upon the anticipated requirement of seating.

5. Decide the pricing of products and services and think about the determinant of such pricing

6. Identify the necessity of any marketing budget and mode of doing such publicity in the target market. This primarily involves deciding how to start a business in a specific market.

7. Use appropriate processes and hierarchy of customer feedback and complaints resolution. Use the feedback constructively to improve the quality of offerings and develop customer-centric solutions

8. Prepare employees' hiring and retention plan

Ideally, you should make a sketch of your business plan on an excel spreadsheet and try to fill your thought in numeric terms on the pointer as mentioned above.

To give you an example of a business sketch for an IT and design start-up, you may look at the following head of income and expenses (these are just indicative and not exhaustive):

Income	Expenses
Website design	Designers and developers
Mobile application	Office rent
IT support	Computers and accessories
Template designs	Test equipment
UI/UX design	Software and licenses
Software design	CA/legal/ Accounting/GST
Logo and brand identity	Staff welfare
	Night charges

	Travel and conveyance
	Electricity charges
	Miscellaneous

So what I mean here is that you must make a rough calculation of the monthly sustenance money your business will need as revenue and how much time you will need to sell those revenue units of products or services. What if you could not bring the required sales for the first few months? The difference of income and expenditure must be in your pocket right away else you will have to take a U-turn after burning your small risk capital.

This rough sketch must answer the following questions for you:

- What will it cost to get your business off the ground?

- How and from where will you get the primary capital for your start-up?

- What are the initial and ongoing expenses of your business? What all are compulsory and optional expenses?

- What is the break-even revenue numbers you need and what gestation period you can afford looking at the financial resources you have?

What is the earning potential of the business once it is fully operational or has achieved 100% or 50% of the set targets? We call it sensitivity analysis wherein we take various incomes and expenses possibilities and analyze our way outs in these circumstances.

How will you bridge the financial gap between the starting stage and break-even stage working capital requirements? Is your money enough or do you need someone to stand with you?

Preserve all your workings of these scenario analysis calculations as these will be needed when you compare them with the actual working and make real business plans and future projections.

Chapter 1.6

The Legality of Your Business

In today's world of global education, creativity, cultural convergence and ever-increasing liberal thoughts, the idea for a business can come from anywhere, without practical or real analysis of the macro and microeconomic factors.

I have come across many business presentations wherein the idea resonates well with the best of economics but the same is either illegal or close to illegality. Even a bleak chance of your business being against the laws of the land can make your business ineligible for funding and prone to early failure.

Though I cannot share how to get conclusive feedback on whether your business idea is legit or not, you should Google for primary view, look deeply into your competitors' websites and their online presence, read the common laws of the country and put the morality perspective into the idea. In the end, analyze without any bias whether your business puts any stakeholder at a short-term or long-term disadvantage. By stakeholder here I mean to include your pool of customers and distributors/suppliers/partners too.

Check the idea thoroughly, including necessary divergences, expansions and ancillaries through the legal lenses. You may take legal help or discuss your idea with one of your friends who may have knowledge of such matters as early as possible. If such primary opinions make it doubtful, then you must take a professional opinion or choose to execute your idea in a different region or country where it is legal. In those situations, you may plan to route the business through that country in such a way that business becomes legal.

You must also get the IPR data for any possible infringement of copyright or trademark. While you name your business, you may do a simple trademark search to avoid the names/contents/processes that bear a conflicting similarity with that of the other registered names or processes. The infringement of other rights can be a breaking situation for your business if you notice the same after you have built a reputation in the market. This is something that will not hit you as long as your business is small in size and is away from the competitor's attention. So, beware of this IPR infringement risk and get your name and trademark registered legally at the earliest.

Such kind of legal opinions by qualified legal professionals and the IPR availability for your process (keep the copy of IPR search reports with you) and names make your business suitable for fund houses to invest. Any idea or mark that has no similarity with existing rights is likely to be not contested in the registrar office, and thus it is good for your business viability, and this saves costs for the business in the near future.

Another tool for checking the legality of your business around the globe is to launch a crowdfunding platform for your business (for very small equity may be or you may choose not to accept money) after you have commenced the business and taken care of your IPR registration.

Just to give you a small example, the business of gambling is illegal in India, but these days, fantasy gaming and pool games (quite near to gambling) are spreading everywhere based on small interpretation support from the judiciary in India, but this business is fully legal in many other countries. Now, as there is a feeble line that decides whether your business is legal or illegal, despite being a unique idea with lucrative financial estimates and growth path, the investor may be more cautious and sceptical in investing in your business. So, what I suggest here is that you take a close look at the negatives and positives and decide what suits you better or how you can mitigate an existing legal risk. Do not be either afraid or super excited about your new idea. Just do your homework fully and learn to understand and note the legal risk and a mitigation plan for the same.

Chapter 1.7

The Similarity of Business Model

In today's world of the internet, which allows us to share information at a fast pace, and the availability of search engines like Google, it is very easy to search similar business models operating in the country or any other part of the world too.

There could be certain comparison issues due to the differences in climate, culture, economic and social status, but the strength and weakness analysis could be simulated in a new set of variables in your geography.

This can be helpful because despite having the first-mover advantage, the risk of launching a new product and making new marketplace are challenging issues. If you have an idea about the market behaviour and SWOT (strength, weakness, opportunity, threat), it shall help you shape the launch and development of your business in your territory.

If you analyze these business models and follow a standard line of comparison, you could also, to a large extent, see the future of your business in the present geography and make action points to overcome issues, if any, in advance.

Always remember that it is difficult to be number one, but it is even more difficult to maintain that position in the face of fierce competition from competitors. It takes a lot to continue to remain at the top.

If a similar business has been doing bad, learn from the same and simulate the business model by changing the offerings and other operational parameters. If a similar business is doing great, then try to optimize the resources to add value to your business, and who knows a bigger company might show interest in investing or acquiring your company soon. In fact, try to learn from both the successes and failures of others and that is the magic of smart learning.

You can innovate a similar business model on the following three fronts:

1. Reinvent the wheel and project your model as the superior one

2. Adapt the core and by simulating the core value in the new situation, make a new core value of the business

3. Revolutionize the core value of the business in such a way that it gets the competitive edge over the present one

So checking out a similar business in another part of the world without having the fear of competition serves to form an outline of the business, provided you also check the intellectual property right protection in your geography.

So, while the first-mover advantage gives you an edge over the existing competition, the last mover is not bad either as it gives you technological and other advantages to be a better company with a higher sustainable quotient.

Chapter 1.8

License and Registration Requirement

In general, countries regulate their economies through registration and licenses to create a congenial and controlled environment for businesses to flourish in a disciplined way.

These may look like a hurdle in simple interpretation, but these are the backbone for new businesses at least because even our biggest competitors have to follow certain regulatory practices to maintain healthy competition and ensure an environment of coexistence.

Registration and licensing cover various aspects, such as identity, registration and basic business framework.

These registration requirements primarily depend upon the following three factors:

1. **Structure of your organization**: Check whether you need to run a proprietorship business or partnership or LLP or LLC. The regulation shall vary and you can either take the help of

the internet to gather basic information or meet an expert for guidance.

2. **Geography of operation:** To run your business in a particular state, you need to comply with the state laws and then central laws. For example, registration under the Shop and Establishment Act depends upon the place or location of your business, on the other hand, income tax, which falls under the category of the central law, applies to your business irrespective of the location. Also, please decide whether you want to transact within India or outside India as you will need an EXIM code for the export and import of goods.

3. **Nature of your business:** The nature of your business shall decide what all local and central registration and licenses you might need. For example, if you run a food business, then along with other registrations you will need an FSSI registration.

Now, there could be registrations that are based on the amount of invoicing you do in a year. In case you cross a certain threshold of billing, you may require a GST registration as well.

A few of the registrations needed are based on the number of manpower employed and the prevailing labour laws. These include PF and ESI registration and welfare funds, among others.

Some registrations are based on the type of organization structure you choose. For example, a limited liability company requires registration under the Companies Act of India, on the other hand, in the case of proprietorship, you do not need that.

One of the most important registrations that is generally overlooked is the IPR registration (at least trademark).

Some registrations could be more of database registration and are recommendatory in nature. This may be government or non-government. For example, registration with an MSME organization (the government of India) or with Dun and Bradstreet (non-governmental). This registration helps you with business growth and marketing network.

Chapter 1.9

Check Your Marketplace

One of the crucial components of a successful business is the availability of an effective market for proposed goods/services.

If you are the first mover, then do proper research on the available marketplace, otherwise, consider aspects such as innovation and adaptation of the presently available product/service. In both situations, you must gauge the size, nature and growth of your target market.

The market size becomes far more important if you ever need to raise funds for your business. It is one of the most basic queries every potential investor is going to ask and even your friends and family should be asking about it during their friendly discussion with you regarding the seed money.

Gathering relevant data depends upon the nature of your product or service. For example, if you are making a toothbrush, then the population of the country or maybe global population can be your customer, but if you are planning on providing income tax return filing services in India, then you need data of people who earn more than the minimum threshold of tax-free income.

The latest population census and organic growth/decline rate of the population can be good sources. Later, you can simulate this data depending upon other input factors like age, earning, education, etc. that may affect the demand.

The number of potential customers or unit sales is one variable, whereas how much that is worth in terms of revenue is a completely different aspect, and perhaps it is more important. You need to know how much revenue that market has to offer before you could decide what market share you can aim for.

Please note the following points for calculating the addressable market size for your business:

1. Define the target audience accurately else all the research on the data gathering and projection of market size shall be rejected without even being read by any investor.

2. The available market size is different from the addressable market size. Apply your product utility and see what percentage of the addressable population can fall for it.

3. No business can aim for 100% of market shares therefore it is good to understand your business scale and horizon. Even investors like big numbers, running in billion dollars, but not the inflated ones. So be cautious while presenting a big number.

4. If you are a good start-up, then probably 2-5% of available market share can be a bullish expectation and up to 1% can be said to be realistic. These market shares percentages are not sacrosanct and are subject to time duration and multiple other factors. The conversion of the available population to your customer-base

depends upon many other variables and the nature of necessity for your product and services.

5. Always count organic growth and not the inorganic windfall gains. A few examples of inorganic growth include your competition getting wiped out for some reason, acquisition of smaller competing businesses, governmental mandates, etc. These are good schemes for exponential growth but these thoughts can be disastrous if one is planning the revenue and sustainability of business on these extraordinary and non-recurring events.

6. Always maintain and preserve your source of information for overall market size estimation and method of deducing your market share before throwing any data on business growth to any investor and try to adopt a conservative approach. A conservative approach towards the key factors of your business shall always help you, irrespective of the stage of business.

Chapter 1.10

The Need for a Co-founder

Now that you have decided to start your business, the next step I recommend is to find a companion to share the journey. While it may seem tempting to control all company decisions or own all the shares in a company, it is important to put your ego aside and invite co-founders to join you in your business.

You anyway cannot be or claim to be so balanced that you can think artistically and be best in number crunching too. We all are, with a few exceptions, either right-brained or left-brained therefore we cannot have the best of both worlds. You are suggested to balance your business by having in-house complementary skills in the form of your co-founder. For example, if you are a technology person and are looking to enter into a FinTech business, it is advisable to have a co-promoter who comes from a finance and business administration background.

Unless you have started with your spouse (or copreneurs), you must try to find at least one person who could complement your skill sets and with whom you could share the happiness of achieving a milestone or the pain of being broke.

Now let me give you a few examples as to why you should consider one or two co-founders:

1. It can save you in all those areas where you lack education or expertise. In the absence of such a partner, you may end up either making mistakes or spending a large amount of money to get that expertise.

2. It will mitigate the risk of losses as the co-founder too will be investing some amount of capital and expertise along with his/her network for funding and marketing.

3. In the name of a co-founder, you also get the privilege to have a sounding board free of cost. It is wise to ask for the opinions of your co-founder on all important strategic decisions and learn to convince the co-founder or get convinced.

4. It increases your bandwidth for your start-up because the co-founder is not an ordinary employee but a person who, just like you, loves the idea and has decided to put the best of his/her ability. You can double up your bandwidth and be at two places at one point in time.

5. If chosen wisely and partnered on the basic philosophy of trust and respect for each other rather than just mitigating the risk and having more money to burn, a co-founder can play a vital role during the tough time in business. Also, this is a simple fact that you will have somebody to stand with you against any third party adversary.

I suggest and believe that a start-up business should have three to four co-founders rather than the common figure of one to two. If this sounds crazy to you, then you may look up numerous success stories wherein the founding CEOs had more than three co-founders.

I must warn you here that no good comes for free, so be wise in delivering the title of co-founder and do a proper compatibility test before you sign off the deal. Maybe you could hire someone based on the commitment of making him/her the co-founder and giving some equity against the delivery of free service or discounted salary, etc.

A wrong decision while choosing a co-founder has the capacity to ruin all your hopes in one go. For any reason, if you happen to have a wrong partner, then get rid of that person at the earliest possible moment but remember to do it on mutually agreeable terms reduced in writing. You must ward off the litigation with your co-founder at all costs and more specifically before you go to investors for raising money. The equity table and legal relationship should be crystal clear and duly sorted for any internal share transfers among such co-founders before raising any institutional fund.

Chapter 1.11

Why Your Business May Fail

If your start-up succeeds, you must be lucky, as you have been able to do what other 90% of people like you could not do. Though luck played a crucial role in the success of Google and Microsoft, there were many humble reasons that assured the success of these companies. 10% of the success of a business depends on how great your idea is, but the rest of 90% always depends upon the execution-style and operational wisdom.

A high passion and drive can definitely help you to ease the initial hiccups a start-up faces but it cannot ensure long-term sustainable growth.

Without getting into subjectivity and behavioural science, let's see the top reasons for the failure of a new business.

The followings are the top 10 reasons for the initial level of failure in the order of their importance and impact:

1. No need for the product or services your business proposes in the market. Essentially, if your business model fails to solve the problems of your target customer, then you are bound to get doomed.

2. Financial constraints can also hamper the success of the new business, so I suggest you conduct a thorough study and plan your finances accordingly. In some cases, founders start focusing too much on the expansion of the business than the revenue generation. Create a bigger market-size with deals and quality deliverables, not with discounts on the prices and other expensive promotion methodologies. Discounting the price and making your product cheaper does not help in the long run.

3. The lack of a competent leader and a qualified team

4. The lack of innovation and customer-centricity. Your business should first talk about the customers' profits and liquidity than yours.

5. Pricing issues and losing customers to bigger players due to the absence of USP (unique selling proposition)

6. Launching your business at the wrong time and the lack of marketing communication. Untimely or delayed launches tend to fail.

7. Disharmony among investors, leader, founder, or the team

8. Lack of passion and self-drive in founders

9. Legal hassles and regulatory restrictions. It could result due to a loss of operational discipline and a lack of understanding of the regulatory environment.

10. The work-life imbalance of the promoter and scalability becoming a challenge. Here the founder and leader find themselves in a unique situation of non-delegation and scalability becomes a challenge.

These top 10 reasons constitute around 99% of the overall reasons for the failure of a business. Learning from your own mistakes as well as the mistakes made by others is crucial in ensuring the success of your business.

The central government and state governments of India have launched various schemes to support the growth of the start-up ecosystem, and over the last three years multiple MNCs also have come up with their own incubators. Being the third-largest start-up ecosystem in the world and one of the largest consumer markets, India has numerous start-ups working in industries ranging from FinTech to FoodTech, Artificial Intelligence and machine learning pivots.

So while you need to be cognizant of the risk of failure, you also need to be aware of the environment and multiple facilities starting from incubators to investors and mentors.

Legal issues in cryptocurrencies forced multiple start-ups in the Indian ecosystem to shut down, and this is a good example to learn as to how legality and regulatory affairs can kill start-ups very early.

So while the reasons for failures are known to us on the macro level, let's summarize some learning from the start-ups in recent times in the context of the Indian market.

- Innovation is the key to the success and growth of start-ups in India. Start-ups need to leverage talent pool, government initiatives and other ecosystem enablers and mentors to innovate and make India a leader rather than a follower.

- Copying solutions and models from successful start-ups/ businesses abroad will eventually lead to failure if these are not customized to the need of the Indian market and business context.

- A business should never be launched without adequate, sound and objective market research. The overestimation of the market and/or underestimation of competitors will only prove detrimental to a start-up.

- Start-ups must be willing to be dynamic and flexible to evolve and sustain in the dynamic business and market environment.

- The founder and promoters must understand their weaknesses faster and onboard experts (including legal and financial consultants) and mentors accordingly in order to ensure that they are not wasting their precious resources and time.

Chapter 1.12

Risk, Opportunity and Plan B

Please know that fewer than one in a thousand start-ups meet or exceed their projected revenues in the planned period. So the capital invested in the start-up business always stands at a high risk whether it is yours or investors.

While you ideate and preview the business model, always count the risk factors involved in all businesses and then specific risks related to your specific business idea.

In general, we can count the following 11 types of risks:

- Management risk
- Business stage risk
- Political/legislative risk
- Manufacturing risk
- Sales and marketing risk
- Funding risk
- Technology risk
- Competition risk
- Litigation risk
- Global risk
- Reputation risk

Now, I want you to help yourself by trying to understand the three biggest risk factors for your business out of the above 11 risks and make a plan to avoid or mitigate the same. This will help sustain your business model and your investor will be comforted to note your wisdom.

Whenever investors come across a good idea, the next thing they want to know is the amount of risk involved so that they can make up their minds on the mode/quantum of investment and exit strategies that interest them. So you could help them by serving that information on a platter.

For mitigating the risks, you could propose few alternate models based on sensitivity analysis, scenario analysis, decision tree and probability distribution. In the end, you should be able to showcase that risks are not only counted, but you are also ready to counter the same as and when it hits your business.

You could also talk to a few insurance companies if the business or IPR could be protected through insurance policies. Though in India, many risks are yet to become insurable, but in many developed countries, those risks could be insured for better stability. For example, the political risk does not get covered by insurance companies in India, but risk covers for the same are available in countries like the USA.

You should not forget to present your plan concerning the 'keyman' or key person insurance and general liability insurance to safeguard your business against any unforeseen loss of key resources or a third party claims.

There are even methods for valuing the start-up that is totally dependent upon the associated risk. Berkus's method of valuation talks about assigning USD 250K for each stage completion, and by stage completion, they mean the reduction of risk. In India, you may read USD as INR for benchmarking purposes.

For example, if the prototype is ready then it means that the technology is sound and technology risk is mitigated. If there is a quality management team, then count the reduction in execution risk, etc.

In short, you must apply your intelligence and wisdom to understand the three biggest risks or the three key factors to successfully establish your business.

If you are excited to know about plan B, then I am sorry to say that you are not yet ready to launch your start-up business. We always think of plan B when we doubt our idea or we lack the willpower to fight the uncertainties of business.

I have mentioned earlier that running a start-up is a rollercoaster ride, and you will end up experiencing myriad emotions on this journey. This is not to scare you but to prepare you for a better tomorrow.

Being ambitious is good, but it is equally important to be aware of the fact that there are 90% chances that you will fail. You need to make informed decisions at every step. You need to know that there is a huge possibility of failure, but at the same time success is not impossible. If you believe that you can do it, and then it becomes a huge strength for you.

If you already know the worst possibilities and you are still determined to do it, then this is how you learn to defeat all the negative forces in your journey. Your product may not be great,

sometimes the customers may complain, you might get a tax notice, you might run out of funds, your friends shall tease you and the best of your employee might leave you. What matters here the most is the fact that you started this alone and you can always reconstruct all the pillars.

The three biggest mistakes that you might end up making before you jump off the cliff are as follows:

1. You do not have a vision as to why you want to start your own business. You have to have immense passion and love for your business and this cannot be challenged at all.

2. You are not ready on the personal front. This may include, taking care of your basic home affairs, your responsibilities towards your dependents and the initial fuel to take off your business.

3. You do not know your strengths and weaknesses and that of your co-founder and teammates who are ready to take the plunge on your command. Before you commence your business, everyone in your team must have crystal clear accountability and action points. Your confidence in your team and your delegation skills start before you commence your business.

Though I mentioned earlier that there are fair chances of failure, there should be no plan B in your mind or the minds of your key people because it has the power to drag you all towards it and make you fail. Believe me that even if your business fails that is not the end of the world because you may get another chance to commence your new business with someone or someone might fund your next start-up and then this experience shall prove to be most helpful. Your failed attempts at running your start-up can teach you things that a management course teaches in three years. It is important to accept the failure with grace and move on.

These days, you can even get hired if you have the experience of running a start-up that failed. The world respects the spirit of entrepreneurs and this line of thought is growing at a fast pace in developed economies, and as you know, developing economies always learn the model of hiring from developed countries.

I will see you in Section 2 of the book when you have commenced your business. Best of luck!

Section 2

THE FIRST 1000 DAYS

Chapter 2.1

Business Structure and Registration

Congratulation on your new start-up!

Now that you have decided to explore your potential to change your own world or maybe the world overall, I welcome you to a life of uncertainties and the elite club of entrepreneurs.

The first issue that you will come across is the structure of the business organization you choose. Every option has its pros and cons, so I leave this decision to your intelligence and wisdom. There are four primary types of organizations as mentioned below:

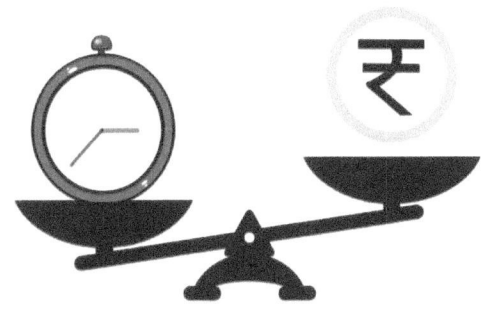

1. **Sole proprietorship:** This type of business is owned by a single person, and it generally requires no registration except opening a bank account in the name of your business. Your PAN is valid for the proposed business and no additional income tax registration is required.

2. **Partnership firm:** Here you sign a deed of partnership and based on that you can apply for a PAN with the income tax department. The partnership firm is treated separately from its partners for income tax purposes. Similar to a sole proprietorship, you do not need to fulfil any registration requirements for the commencement of your business. Besides, the partnership deed can also be registered in the district court or Registrar of Firms. However, the liabilities of partners are unlimited, and this is the main issue with this structure. A partnership firm is not a separate legal entity and the existence/continuance of such business depends entirely upon the survival/willingness of partners.

3. **Limited Liability Partnership (LLP):** This is an advanced version of partnership wherein the registration is done with the Registrar of Companies and the liabilities of partners are made limited subject to few terms as per the Limited Liability Partnership Act. Since LLP is treated as a firm, no minimum alternate taxes and dividend distribution taxes are levied. The remuneration to partners and interest on capitals can be paid as per the law.

4. **Limited Liability Company (LLC):** This is the most refined version of a privately held business and the registration process is adopted as per the Companies Act 2013. The company is treated as a separate legal entity, which means that the company is separate from its shareholders and compliances/restrictions are applicable as per the law. The liabilities of shareholders are limited to the subscription of shares only. Setting up an LLC is complicated as compared to all other forms of business organizations. However, it is imperative to note that any business that is ready for expansion and seeks to attract investors and talented manpower is generally incorporated as LLC.

We will read about LLC and its compliances and management in detail in our next chapter. We also call LLC as PLC (private limited company) when the shares of the company are held by a small number of people rather than the public at large.

One of the most contentious issues that budding entrepreneurs struggle with is whether to start an LLC or LLP. Though there are various similarities between the two, LLP is a hybrid model with limited liability features, lesser compliance, and a higher degree of flexibility in operation as compared to LLC. If you are an entrepreneur who needs external funding, more equity participants and aims to get into the global market, then a private limited company is the perfect business structure for you.

FDI is allowed in both structures but as of now, external commercial borrowing is not allowed in LLP. So, LLP is a better option when more than one person with limited capital is entering into a business and one does not foresee multiple partners and frequent exchange of shareholding and ownerships.

Now I assume that you have already validated your idea and decided on the corporate structure, so the followings are the initial action points:

1. Set up a timeframe for getting your business registered. It does not matter much but it is preferable to have a limited liability company registered, which is not a costly affair these days as it does not require any registration charges and has comparable compliance cost, etc. PLC is a preferred structure for investors and their future exit strategies. In addition, they will like to invest in large format business than a closed group.

2. The incorporation of a company shall require a minimum of two directors and two shareholders. I assume that by now you must have decided the shares of your co-founder if any, and so I do not need to say more. But it is wise to keep at least a simple majority (51%) with you for better control in any future decision

making. Choose your other director wisely as the person should be available during the board meeting and signing of company documents. If you have a co-founder then no issue, or else make your parent or spouse the other director for now. If you do not have a co-founder, then allot 1% of shares to your spouse or parent (other directors) and keep the rest of 99% with you. It may be helpful to you when you want to bring somebody else into the company. Also, it is important to note that the director of the company may not be a shareholder. The shareholder and director can be a different set of people. Even for LLP, the requirements for registration remain similar but with different nomenclature.

3. You will need to create your brand identity and logo, print stationeries like visiting cards and letterhead, brochure, etc. and establish the digital presence of your business through a website and social media accounts. You may also like to announce your new venture on your own social media account. Keep the personal email as the master email for links and recovery for the time being as the same can be changed later when you have dedicated hosting space.

   Now, while the above steps are progressing, make your milestones for product development and enlist the people who can support you with their money. Also, make a list of people who should be your prospective clients. Just pull up each number from your mobile on an excel sheet and write what he/she can do for you in your present business set-up. Call the relevant people and go and meet them at their convenience. Be sure not to bug your contacts too much. Out of the list of people in your network, target 10 people to share your business idea with as an investment proposition.

4. Get your finances in the bank and proceed for the liquidation of any stock, mutual fund or other assets that are not in liquid form. At times, this process might take your precious time.

5. I suppose within two weeks you should be ready with your company registration (or LLP), PAN (Permanent Account Number) and TAN (tax deduction account number). Unlike earlier days, PAN and TAN are automatically granted (not available for LLP as of now) by the income tax department along with company registration these days and you do not need to apply separately.

6. Now you need to open the company's current account with a bank. The bank may be chosen as suggested by the professional who helped you incorporate the company, or you can choose a bank that is nearest to your home or in which you or your parents already have an account and good rapport. What I suggest here is that it is better to have a direct relationship with the banker or through someone for the initial troubleshooting.

7. Now everything looks sorted and you are ready to launch yourself in the market. Search for start-up meeting places or investor clubs in your city. These meetings generally happen at co-working places of repute. Keep a tab on them and sign up for all such events. After attending a few such meetings, you will understand how to approach the investors with your business offering and the necessity of funds.

Chapter 2.2

Company and Compliances

I suppose now you are serious about your business, eyeing big potential to grow, contemplating funding and foreign investment, etc., and you have decided to incorporate your private limited company for your impactful presence. It is important to know the little details and  compliance structure about the management of a private limited company.

The basic idea of this chapter is to acquaint the readers with the salient features, basic dos and don'ts, compliances and periodicity under the Companies Act 2013. The chronological compliances for PLC are as follows:

1. Filing of commencement of business (Form INC20A) with the registrar of companies. This can be done within 180 days since the incorporation but the sooner, the better as you cannot commence your business without this. Non-filing attracts penalties on the company and directors.

2. The appointment of the auditor has to be done within 30 days of the incorporation of the company and a related form (ADT-1)

to be filed within the next 15 days of such appointment. The first appointment shall be for five years.

3. Within 30 days of the incorporation, the first board meeting should happen, and thereafter a minimum of four such meetings should be conducted in a year. The maximum gap between the two board meetings should not exceed 120 days.

4. Annual general meeting (AGM) to be conducted within nine months from the closing of the first financial year, and thereafter within six months of the closing of Financial Years (FY) for subsequent FY. The gap between the two AGM should not exceed 15 months.

5. Every director must disclose their interests in all board meetings and any specific items and disclosures/declarations should be made every financial year in appropriate forms.

6. For every annual general meeting, a 21-day notice should be given to shareholders along with the details of the agenda and an explanatory statement concerning any special business to be transacted at such a meeting.

7. A financial statement should be filed with the Registrar of Companies within 30 days of the conclusion of the annual general meeting.

8. The annual returns of the company should be filed within 60 days of the conclusion of AGM.

9. A statutory audit must be done every year by a qualified chartered accountant (CA) irrespective of the turnover of the business.

10. The company must maintain few statutory registers in the prescribed format such as the register of members, register of charges, register of directors and key managerial personnel, register of loans and guarantee, etc.

11. Minutes of the board meeting and general meeting, Attendance Register, Books of Accounts, etc. are to be maintained at the registered office of the company.

12. Filing of appropriate forms as and when any change in share capital, mortgage and other substantial activity happens. Generally, these are due within 30 days of such an event.

13. The company cannot accept loans from any individual who is not the Director of the company. Loans from the Director is allowed, provided such Director declares that he/she has not taken any personal loan to give the same to the company.

14. A loan from shareholders is allowed only when the company is not a subsidiary or associate of any other company. It is also important to make sure that the company is not indebted for more than Rs. 50 crores or twice of paid-up capital (whichever is lower) and has not defaulted on the repayment of such loans from the bank and other financial institutions.

15. Depositing cash in the company's account should be completely avoided unless you can present the audit trails and justify such deposits. Lesser cash withdrawal and the non-payment of cash (except petty cash) shall be helpful to the company in multiple ways.

16. Maintain proper records and preserve copies of all sales and purchase invoices and evidence of expenses. The income should be fully recognized irrespective of its absence in your tax credit statement (26AS).

For delay in filing of forms, the penalty shall be charged on delayed filing and the company as well as an officer (in default) may be penalized or prosecuted depending upon the severity of the offence.

All the above-mentioned compliances are as per the Companies Act 2013 and compliances under other relevant applicable laws are as follows:

- Payment of periodic tax dues (GST, TDS & TCS)

- Filing of periodic returns (monthly, quarterly, annual returns) such as TCS/TDS/GST

- Assessment of advance tax liability and payment of advance tax in a proportionate manner (15% by June 15; 45% by Sept 15; 75% by Dec 15 and 100% by March 15)

- Payment of final self-assessment income tax and filing of income tax returns as per the appropriate ITR form

- Filing of Tax Audit Report if a tax audit is applicable. The tax audit slabs keep changing. Currently, it is applicable on turnover worth Rs. 1 crore (5 crores if less than 5% cash transaction).

- Payment of PF and ESI dues if applicable and filing of periodic returns

It is advisable to hire a consultant to take care of all these compliances, but it is equally important to receive the compliance report from the consultant on a regular basis so that you could correct the mistakes and cure the non-compliances well within the timeline.

I have come across many businesses in which tax consultants educate the owners as to how to avoid tax, pay lower tax by showing extra expenses and get the refunds on the income tax deducted by clients on the sales invoices. Though you can benefit from getting some quick money back in a short period, this approach is not advisable as you may fail to justify your tax returns in the case of ITR scrutiny. In addition, it will affect your reputation in the long-run if an investor finds out that you are making a profit using methods that are below the industry standards.

Thus, by taking these shortcuts, you are likely to ruin the financial credentials of your own business and make it handicapped to even raise capital later from banks or other investors.

Chapter 2.3

Seed Fund and Primary Capital

As the word suggests, seed funding is the seed capital based on which the revenue tree of business grows and gives fruit in terms of profit. Barring few ventures wherein the business fails or does below average, the seed money investor always gets high returns as compared to any conventional investment on the capital invested.

I suggest the seed should be your own hard-earned savings or the support money from your part-time earning during the gestation period.

Along with investing money for the first three months, you must also bounce off the idea with your immediate family unless you fear the confidentiality issue from their side due to the lack of maturity or internal competition. If you have the buy-in for running the business for three months, you should offer small equity participation to those early investors and an early exit if they want so, or you may  offer buyback of their shares at the very first stage of any funding (also known as liquidity event). This will make them feel happy and less risky.

Rather than taking bulks of money from one person, you should try taking small sums from different groups of people as they would also become the foot soldiers for the initial word of mouth publicity.

When you are lucky, the professional angel/seed investor too would like to invest in your business in the form of a loan or convertible instruments, but these investments generally happen in the category of promoters, and investors play an important role in growing the company and developing products from scratch level. The only catch is that since they are involved in running the business and are investing money as well, you might end up losing substantial ownership to them. Also, you must keep in mind that while you are into this business because you love the idea, the professional investor is here for the love of higher return on investment (ROI). So, the line of thought may be very different if not radical.

 Even though there is an ever-growing number of seed capital funds in the market, it is believed that raising seed funds is the toughest task of all and more so when you are a first-time entrepreneur or have no history of any other successful start-up. So, while there is no scarcity of places where you can apply for seed funds but, at the same time, getting funded is a difficult feat to achieve.

Here are the reasons why this seed round is the most difficult round and a few standard ways to ease those difficulties:

1. There could be many followers once you have a lead investor who is convinced of your idea and ready to fund you. However, for a lead investor, it is a work that requires due diligence for a small quantum of investment and involves lots of responsibilities towards the follow-on investors. All you could do here is follow

the advice of preparation and business research and leave only a small amount of work for the lead investor.

2. How much equity for how much money? In general, the founders either under-price or overprice the equity as the prospect of the idea and its future is subjective. The angel investor thinks that it is his money that is at stake, on the other hand, the founder thinks that it is his idea that is more important. The founder tries to maintain the majority shareholding until a few billion comes into his own bank account. This creates a huge difference between the way a founder and an investor think, and as a result, the deal does not go through either at the valuation or the terms sheet level. All I can suggest here is to have multiple rounds of discussion and value the seed capital as the primary pillar of the start-up and you may ease your expectations a bit or get into some kind of staggered or milestone-based funding. Milestone-based funding is not best suited for start-up businesses, but instead of accepting a no, it is better to have a source of credit available to you, when you are confident about the success and a good ROI for investors.

3. Going beyond the seed fund round, the founder hopes to find a professional angel investor who can be a force-multiplier in his/her business. One of the common issues at this stage, which happens due to lack of manpower, is the failure to implement suggestions from lead investors on matters like board formation, advisory boards, structuring the investment, process update and MIS. The founder is always busy getting the core manpower and product line developed and so generally forget about the requirement of investors which can make further funding difficult even if you have been funded at the seed level. It is important for founders to understand that while followers are large in numbers and lead investors are few, the lead investors

who can be force-multipliers for the founder need to be always satisfied for his model to work in the favour of the organization.

Here is my advice on seed capital arrangement,

- Invest some of your money
- Borrow the double of the amount invested by you from friends and family
- Within three months of the first infusion, keep looking for another set investor (friends and family extension) who can pay at least double of last raised fund
- Look for an angel investor who can carry all expenses for further one year till you get funding from a venture capital firm
- Keep the progress chart always ready on a monthly basis
- Keep giving possible and practical exits to early investors if they look for that

Chapter 2.4

Making a Prototype or Proof of Concept (POC)

A prototype is the release of a product with the purpose of testing the built, logic, semantic and usability of the ideated product. It is considered as the primary stage of the product evaluation for mass usage.

This is an important step towards making the investment a worthy proposition for big investors. Irrespective of the business stage, this is an important preparation towards the completion of the product cycle, which should be done as soon as possible and without waiting for any round of funding. The sooner this happens, the better it is. It gives requisite confidence to all the stakeholders, whether it is you or your family or your professional investor group or even employees.

By prototype, we mean the conversion of your idea on paper into physical reality. Tech ideas are known as 'prototype', whereas non-tech ideas are known as a proof of concept (POC). However, a proof of concept is also taken as a revenue model assumption for tech businesses, which is a stage after developing the prototype.

In order to bring your ideas to life, it is important to give birth to a highly visual product that communicates and represents all your ideas and goals and provides basic interactive functionalities. In this case, a prototype act as a perfect solution for transferring your ideas and vision in the form of a product that can be both seen, and, more importantly, experienced by those involved.

Google Ventures design partner Daniel Burka says, *"The ideal prototype should be of Goldilocks quality. If the quality is too low, people won't believe the prototype is a real product. If the quality is too high, you'll be working all night, and you won't finish. You need Goldilocks' quality. Not too high, not too low, but just right."*

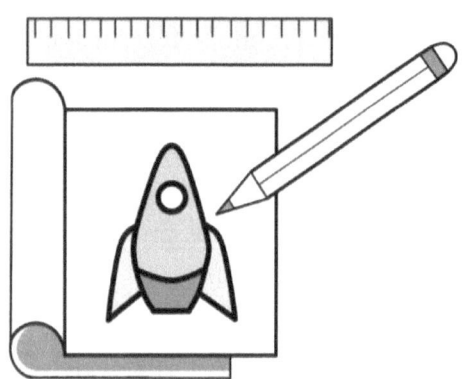

In fact, an idea alone cannot be funded except the execution could be guaranteed in one way or another. In such cases, prototyping plays a vital role in removing the business risk of technology and execution. After the prototype stage, the other business process risks like selling, distribution and other financial risks can be analyzed clearly by an investor who knows how to play with these risks or can guide the start-up investee company on these matters. It simply paves the way for the investor to witness the overall horizon of the product and the vision of the founder. This helps you to reduce your documentation and flashy stories of your creativity and shift your focus on those aspects of the business that the seed investors mostly consider before they put their money. By crossing this stage, even the institutional venture funding gets simply expedited both at preparation and presentation level.

You must take note of the following points while making the prototype:

1. Focus on what all to prototype. These can include your customer acquisition, UI/UX, competition differentiator and stories around the idea.

2. Prototyping must validate your idea and should communicate to others that the stage of prototyping takes the technology risk or execution risk far from any apprehended failure.

3. The investor must perceive that you are no more selling the idea about a product but the product itself.

4. The prototype should be of the original idea and it should be at least that of the beta stage and under no circumstance should break while testing. If your prototype does not work during the presentation even for a few seconds, you will be blown out.

5. The prototype should be available for IPR filing, and it should be prepared to an extent that once an investor shows interest, you can initiate the IPR filing immediately and preferably before the next meeting with the investor. You need to have a solid understanding of what you are trying to do before you go and file an application for copyright or patent. The product specification and definition phases set the stage for formal patent/copyright applications.

Prototypes provide a substantial look and feel to your audience about the capabilities of the product. The prototyping process allows you to test product features, operating methods, feedback mechanisms and user experiences before the full-scale operation, and it helps you make the product more refined and innovative. The feedback and information you gather from prototype testing are crucial in implementing and launching a successful product. The faster you prototype, the faster you can test, improve, and launch the product in the market. Rapid prototyping is a great way to shape your idea into an intuitive and user-focused product. In addition, it helps you gain access to the best options available in the competitive world for quicker acquisition of market share or take the first-mover advantage or even get considered for strategic participation from industry leaders. In today's world, it is the prototyping and feedback mechanism that form the base of the agile development of a product through experience and adaptation.

Chapter 2.5

Making the Pitch Deck or IM

Here comes the first stage of preparation for you to get an audience time from investors' circle. As you are not bound by the geography of your operation for funding requirements, so you may send the pitch deck to all the investors communicating your value proposition irrespective of their location.

It is generally believed that the first three slides of your deck decide whether the investor will continue to read the remaining portion of your deck or not. Therefore, it is important to prepare a well-drafted and content-balanced deck. We also call the Pitch Deck, an information memorandum (IM).

The pitch deck is a presentation that an entrepreneur makes for seeking investment, and on an average, this should not include more than 15 slides. To be more precise, your deck should not include less than 10 slides and more than 25 slides.

The business idea in the form of a pitch deck should be clear and compelling enough to convince an investor. It must not be too technical else it will not fly if the desk person is averse to certain areas of technicality. Besides, the words used should be free of technical jargon as much as possible, and the use of visuals is suggested than making the deck text-heavy.

I must quote the pitch deck template that was created by Silicon Valley Legend Peter Thiel, who suggested the inclusion of the following slides in your pitch deck. One could have a maximum of 10% diversion on the contents of slides and the addition of a few essentials, but the skeleton should not be altered much.

1. **Problem statement:** Why this idea, and what problems of society does it solve? This should be communicated in the simplest words. The target audience and investors should be able to relate to the problem without much perusal and discussion. In addition, the investor should find your technical education and expertise useful in solving that problem. For example, if you are an architect and talking about bringing space management in the commercial or residential places through unique furniture designs, the same shall sound much convincing than the same architect talking about data analytics and machine learning.

2. **Solution:** How does the proposed product/service solve those problems? Your product or service being proposed at the right time ticks the box here. The solution should neither be too early or too late. You must also talk about the scalability of the product here.

3. **Market:** The overall market size for your products or services in a defined market place can start from specific geography and extend around the globe. Global markets of less than a few billion USD do not interest investors as they aim to multiply their investment by eight to 10 times in the next three to seven years. You could also use a few projections basis some research with the source of information mentioned therein.

4. **A product that is new or is an improved adaption:** This is all about showcasing your solution. Few live pictures, animation or test results shall talk better, and if you have conducted prototype testing, then the feedback on the functionality of the prototype. The product has to be either new or a smart and improved adaptation of the competitor's product.

5. **Traction/engagement model**: Here the investor shall like to see the traction or engagement model proposed or the level of traction as on date if you have had a beta launch. In case it is too early for you to show these, maybe you could show a dry run data.

6. **Team:** This is again the most important slide because it is not the idea alone that can be a differentiator but successful execution capabilities thereof. More than 100 people may have thought about this idea, but they could not manifest it into action. The team slides should ideally have details on management and the co-founder and all executives/key people. The mention of reasoning as to why they are the best in their respective fields, further backed up by their past achievements, shall make the slide complete. All these should be mentioned using bullet points.

7. **Competition landscape:** You must mention the competition and the point of differentiation. A pictorial or graphical representation suits better. You may also mention how much capital your competitor has already raised and what they have achieved to date. If you could showcase the same level of growth with lesser investment, due to better implementation strategy and product qualities as compared to your competitor, you are likely to hit the bull's eye and gain the attention of investors immediately.

8. **Financial projection and value creation:** You need to provide a summary of financial statements in one of the slides wherein the basic pre-revenue figures/as on date performance or three/five years projected number could be shared. This slide is quite important because it draws a clear picture of the potential of your business in the investor's mind. If you have been too aggressive or too conservative about the growth, then both are killer as you need to adopt a balanced approach. You may also show the scenario analysis to investors. You must always have the financial plan ready in a spreadsheet for showing to investors if they want to get into details of revenue modelling or cash burning and assumption parameters.

9. **The amount being raised and burn plan:** You should mention the amount of investment required in terms of range than an absolute figure so that you could be in the bucket list of more investors. For example, rather than writing Rs. 2 crores, better write Rs. 1 to Rs. 3 crores. Here, a quick macro burn plan shall be helpful for investors and a timeline for raising the next fund too can be mentioned.

According to research conducted by DocSend, on an average, an investor spends three minutes and 44 seconds precisely on each pitch deck and decides whether to consider it for the next round of evaluation or not. They typically spend substantial time on the team, competition and financial statements.

It is a good idea to give your social introduction like sharing LinkedIn or other social media account details so that investors could be sure of your credentials independently, too. It is also advisable to pay attention to the images and colour scheme of your pitch deck. If you are not good at designing these templates, then there is no harm in paying some money and getting makeover assistance from a friend or professional.

Chapter 2.6

Drafting an NDA (Non-Disclosure Agreement)

As the name suggests, this is an agreement that binds anybody who happens to know your idea and solutions with the inherent obligation to not share/disclose the same in an unauthorized way and without your prior consent. This protects you against the copying and piracy or unauthorized use of your idea and solutions.

There are several instances wherein you can sign a non-disclosure agreement (NDA). Keeping our agenda clear, you need to get an NDA signed when you share your idea with anybody including the following:

1. Development partner
2. Investor
3. Distributor/supplier
4. Prospective buyer/licensee
5. Your own partners/employees
6. Your service providers

The NDA could be mutual or single-sided (non-mutual) depending upon the requirement, but in your case, it could be only non-mutual as you are hardly going to get any confidential data from the other end.

However, there is no harm in signing a mutual NDA too if one of the parties insists on doing so.

The following points and clauses must be considered and should be part of the NDA draft:

1. You must include the authorized representatives and employees of the recipient parties in addition to the standard extension of associated individuals or organizations. Basically, cover all the possible third parties who might end up receiving confidential information while you share the same with the main party.

2. The definition of confidential information should be exhaustive and non-exclusive in nature because at the time of signing of this agreement, you never have the full idea of what all information could be shared.

3. Exclusion of NDA should be mentioned even though those exceptions are very common like information which is in the public domain, etc.

4. The terms of the agreement should be mentioned and it should not be less than two years unless a special event occurs. Please make sure to include that even after the expiry of an NDA, the rights covered under intellectual property rights cannot be used by the recipient just because the NDA expired.

5. Non-poaching of employees and non-solicitation of clients may be put as standard terms of an NDA. There could be a situation wherein the receiving party hires your key employee and get

him/her to copy your intellectual properties or even redevelop the same. Non-solicitation of clients too must be covered.

6. The public announcement or taking credit for the existence of such an agreement should be a subject of mutual agreement and should be done by taking prior permission of the disclosing party.

7. Finally, the jurisdiction must be the area where your company operates and not where the recipient party does its business.

8. The agreement should be dated, signed and stamped too if being signed on behalf of the company or entity with full disclosure of the position of the person who is signing it. If the agreement is being signed by one of the employees of a company, you should insist on an authority letter in his/her favour by the director/owner.

Many times, a practical problem arises and you may need to share the concept/pitch deck to people with whom it is not possible nor warranted to get an NDA executed. In that case, summarize the points of NDA and put that in one of the slides of the presentation/pitch deck and write an inclusive language that receipt of the information is covered by terms of non-disclosure obligations. This does your work without making it a big pointer at least in those cases wherein only you are willing to share your business idea without the recipient's invitation.

Chapter 2.7

First Investor Group Meeting

Great, you have crossed all the previous stages! It is now time to have your first meeting with a serious investor. This is the time to make a kill and make your point to the world.

While it is natural to feel excited about this new horizon, I suggest you consider this meeting as one of the many opportunities you will get while you are on this journey of getting funded. So do not spend sleepless nights and do not be nervous.

It is always good to be best prepared and for that, you should consider the following points:

1. Know all the possible details about the investor fund house and their recent investments, successes and failures. Also, research on the person/partner to whom you are going to present. Initially, try to break the ice by engaging in small talks concerning his/her area of interest (like a particular person, technology or country, etc.) but do not sound too accommodating. After doing some research, do not assume that you know everything about the

person but rather try to maintain an air of curiosity to know the person better.

2. Be well-dressed (wear formal clothes even though you are going to present a media or tech concept) and reach the location 10 minutes earlier than the decided time. It shows your seriousness. If you are early, then register your arrival in the system and wait for the call. If due to any unavoidable circumstances you are late, then please seek the prior permission from the person you were to meet and do apologize and thank in the same breath that your delay could be accommodated.

3. Re-check the pitch book and all the essential data and research used in making of pitch book

4. Talk about the idea and then the team. Market and competition come last while you narrate your story. People love stories, so try to make a story that includes facts.

5. Gather all the documents supporting the data in your pitch book in a nice document holder and keep it marked by a separator so that you do not have to search any document under discussion. Keep an extra copy, if possible, as the same may be a good gesture when you offer to leave a copy with investors.

6. Prepare yourself for all the possible tough questions and back up your answers with facts than logic and emotions. Make sure to remain calm and composed. Do not allow tough questions to let you feel demotivated or frustrated in front of the investors and rather appreciate it as an alternate thought.

   Be ready for criticism and thank the investor for that feedback. Acknowledge that his/her feedback is helpful while you innovate the business or for your next upgrade. Thank them with grace as you never know when you will meet the investor again for a different product or purpose.

7. The application of funds must have been shown in the pitch book but try to mention the same additionally indicating that it is the product development or market acquisition, etc. and not the handsome salaries of promoters that will be taken care of by the investment. In addition, it is the right time to prove that the application of funds is wise as well as appropriately measured for the projected ROI.

8. If you have the financial plan ready and it is under discussion, then the working capital gap and Capex outflow must add to the money being asked. If you are not good with numbers, then it is advisable to take the help of your financial advisor or co-founder who knows it better.

9. Do not make the meeting one-sided. It is a give-and-take relationship, so if you have 40 minutes, divide the time equally. Let the investor speak for 20 minutes and share his part of stories and experience. If no relevant question comes to your mind, you may ask for their feedback and their suggestion as veterans of the investment banking and funding world.

10. Do not be a yes-man as nobody likes a spineless CEO of their investee company. The investors are investing money in you as he/she thinks of you as a competent individual, and you must present yourself as someone with a solid backbone and emotional stability. Even the suggestions given by the investor on value improvement of your offerings should be cross-questioned. It is very important to let the investor speak out their mind as the same become the fodder for the next round of meetings. An interactive meeting will leave a good impression on their minds even if you do not get immediate buy-in.

11. Do not give long answers as the same may eat up investor's time and show that you are stubborn and inexpressive about your idea and are not ready for flexibility and dynamism. It is good to

be passionate but do not be a maniac as it may reflect a lack of adaptability.

In a nutshell, if you could satisfactorily demonstrate your business model and an investor could trust your intelligence, dynamism and leadership skill and gives you a roadmap for the further engagement process, it's a successful meeting.

Chapter 2.8

Investor Report

Investors love to receive and see the progress report of the invested companies but without really asking for it. They must know how their portfolios are performing and whether it was a good investment decision or not.

This also helps you to maintain a cordial and regular relationship with the investor, and after taking money from the investor, this should be a moral as well as a professional obligation for entrepreneurs. Besides, these obligations are duly mentioned in the terms sheet and shareholder agreements. Investor relationship management is of prime importance for you and you must never compromise on this.

The report should be straight, simple and to the point. It would be good if you could maintain one static format to make the consumption of contents easier for the investor.

I suggest a monthly frequency of such operational updates, and if, for the bandwidth issue, the same is not possible, quarterly updates are absolutely necessary. You can also choose tools available for real-time reporting, but these methods may not work at times because while it is good to have a proactive approach (like sharing updates), you must also keep a safe harbour for you.

In general, what all an investor would like to know or you would like to share are as follows:

1. The growth matrix and a month-over-month comparison shall be a good piece of information for investors. This may be financial growth, like revenue or expenses or EBIDTA (earnings before interest, depreciation, taxes and amortization).

2. Consumer engagement updates and tractions and results of the action taken in this regard

3. Product enhancement updates/new features added or made operational geographically

4. Any special or big client signed up or any understanding signed up with dealer, distributor, or supplier

5. Any substantial media update, such as newspaper coverage or social media comments/likes, etc.

6. Any investment banking news in a particular industry to whom your business belongs or any new legislation benefitting or affecting your business class

7. Any target milestone achieved or due in the near future before the next report

8. Key employees, key departmental function, individual achievements and R&R programs conducted in the organization

9. Any planned Capex or event of substantial nature towards achieving your final goal

10. Update on the bank balance and burn rate and an estimate of the revenue cycle or the timeline for the next round of funds or break-even moments

11. Any strategic association with other entities or membership of any industry body/association

I do not think that one can really count what all events could be substantial news for a particular business but anything which gives you either pain or pleasure should ideally be updated to investors for their reference.

The investor report should be well-drafted, neat and easy to understand with colours and fonts chosen intelligently and preferably in line with the brand colours.

Chapter 2.9

Intellectual Property Right (IPR) Filing

Intellectual property rights (IPR), in general, are the legal rights/titles for intangible property or assets, created in favour of an applicant/creator. There could be many types of intellectual assets, but generally, these may be as follows:

- Patents
- Trademarks
- Copyrights and related rights
- Industrial designs
- Trade secrets
- Layout design for integrated circuits
- Protection of new plant variety

The above rights can be registered too unlike other types of intangible assets such as goodwill or creditworthiness.

In India, these intellectual property rights are governed by various central legislations like the Trademark Act, Copyright Act, Patent Act/Rules and other allied laws and are administered through the office of Controller General of Patents, Designs & Trade Marks (CGPDTM).

IPR plays a key role in almost every sector and has become a crucial factor for investment decisions by many investors/companies. The well-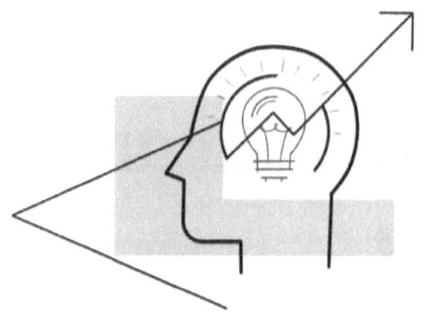balanced IPR regime in India acts as an incentive for foreign players to protect their intellectual property in India. This can be established by the fact that nearly 80% of patent filings in India are from MNCs. In today's highly competitive global economy, IPRs are giving companies a cutting edge against their competitors. With recent changes in IP laws, various IP related issues have sprung up, which are highly complex in nature and need due calibration by new-age entrepreneurs before they decide on the registration requirements.

Now let me give you basic facts and a brief process map for the registration of various IPRs.

1. **Trademark registration**: It is required for the brand name or logo or any unique business mark, etc. Here, first, you do a trademark search to see if a similar trademark is already registered. You will need to file an appropriate form along with the requisite government fee (please note that small companies registered as MSME pay a concessional fee). You must check the various trademark categories and decide what all are best described in your product and service and may be in place of filing under one category, you may end up filing a few more. Each application is treated as a separate application and the fee is payable accordingly. You will also need copies of the trademark duly printed on the plain sheet to be submitted along with the application. If not contested, you can expect the registration of the trademark within six to 12 months.

The trademark registrations are valid for 10 years and are renewable after that period. It is better to take the help of trademark agents whom you can find from the trademark office site or other trademark attorneys

2. **Copyright registration:** This is for all artistic and literary works like music or books or software, etc. The copyright registration is granted for the lifetime of the author (except photographs) and sixty-year post the author's death.

To get the copyright registration the following process should be followed:

- Application (including all the particulars and the statement of the particulars) in the appropriate format of FORM IV has to be sent to the registrar along with the requisite fees. A separate application has to be made for separate works.

- Every application has to be signed by the applicant as well as an attorney in whose favour the power of attorney (POA) has been executed.

- The registrar will issue a Dairy No. followed by a mandatory waiting time for a period of 30 days for any objections to be received.

- If there are no objections received within 30 days, the scrutinizer will check the application for any discrepancy and in case of no discrepancy, the registration will be done and an extract will be sent to the registrar for the entry in the Register of Copyright.

Copyright subsists in a work by virtue of creation hence it is not mandatory to register. However, registering a copyright provides evidence that copyright subsists in the work and the creator is the owner of the work. Creators often give the rights of their works to individuals or companies for production, marketing and distribution, in return for a payment known as a royalty.

3. **Patent registration:** There could be multiple types of patents, but the basic idea remains constant that it should involve novelty and invention. It could be a processor design or utility or plant (agriculture). A patent grants an inventor a legally enforceable monopolistic right over their invention. This means that others can be legally restrained from exploiting the invention. The patent registrations are granted for a period of 20 years.

To get the registration for the patent, you need to apply in an appropriate form along with a fee and unless there is an objection, the patents are grated and sealed if the examiner is satisfied with the novelty/ invention and there is no prior registration for same product or process. For a patent to be granted, the item must not be a prohibited item (like atomic energy) and must be non-obvious and useful.

Among all the IPRs, the patent is complex and costly to register.

Infringement of IPR is punishable as per the governing laws of the country and the aggrieved party can file a complaint and ask for injunctions, damages and penalties, etc.

One obvious question that a lot of people ask is how to protect my idea. The answer to this question is that idea cannot be registered unless manifested in some tangible or intangible form.

So, while a trademark is a basic registration that protects a name or logo, but depending upon the nature of your business, product, artwork, design, process, or invention, you must make the other applicable intellectual property rights application as soon as possible because it is the date of application which matters a lot while deciding the merit of the case and grant of your application.

Chapter 2.10

Financial Planning and Forecasting

Financial planning essentially refers to putting numbers in your strategies and action plan. While there could be a considerable degree of variation in the scope and formalities depending upon the size and explicit time horizon of these planning, most corporate businesses have the following commonality while doing this exercise: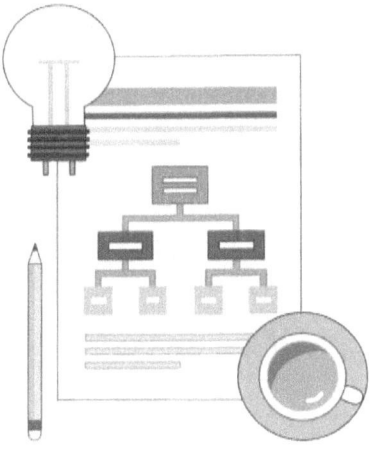

1. Basic assumptions

2. Capital Budgeting (Capex)

3. Operating Cost Budgeting (Opex)

4. Corporate finance: Source of finance both long-term and short-term

5. Pro forma statements of profit and loss account, net worth statement (also named balance sheet more commonly) and cash flow statement

As we invest a lot of time and energy making this plan, which is necessary for internal as well as external use, it is important to know the following benefits of making a financial plan:

a. Scientific forecast of future events

b. Benchmark of performance

c. Check on the viability of strategic plans

d. An alternate dynamic plan readily available when the environment changes

e. Linkage of the present decision with future outcomes

People generally perceive financial planning and analysis in its myopic definition of doing budgeting and variance analysis, but it is much more than that as it is an essential tool for decision-making and not just number crunching.

Financial planning necessarily includes the followings steps:

- Making annual operating plans
- Capital budget and operating cost budgets
- Manpower headcount planning and departmental salary cost budget
- Financial modelling—what if and sensitivity analysis
- Forecasting mechanics and trend review
- MIS and dashboards
- Performance management and KPI
- Variance analysis
- Accountability and incentive planning

It is the complete module for managing the financial performance of a business that is finally linked to the mission and vision of the company.

DD Eisenhower, an American army general and statesman, who served as the 34th president of the United States defended the planning process as, "In preparation of battle, I always found that plans are useless but planning is indispensable. The planning process forces you to think deeply and futuristically in a more systematic manner."

Among forecasting the multiple items of a profit/loss account or balance sheet, the most essential and the starting point is sales forecast and revenue modelling. Sales forecast and revenue modelling are not art that depends upon the thought process of marketing and sales head or business owner but a scientific process wherein data is evolved, derived, deduced and refined.

Sales forecasting can be done using various qualitative and quantitative techniques over and above the best estimate methodology of cause and effect. The followings are commonly used methods of forecasting:

Quantitative	Qualitative
Time series analysis	User survey method
Trend analysis	A panel of expert opinion
GDP growth	Salesforce votes
Market and economy inflation	Delphi Method
Casual techniques	Test marketing
Simulation	Bayesian decision method

The sales forecast is called balanced when it considers the various benefits and limitations of all the possible methods and takes into account the environmental and industry forecast too.

The most basic steps of sales forecasting are as follows:

1. Setting goals for forecasting
2. Gathering various input/data
3. Analyzing the data
4. Selecting the tool for forecasting
5. Forecasting basis the input and methodology
6. Evaluating the forecasting outcomes

The sales forecast should not be confused with the sales budget as it precedes the budget process which consists of production, administrative and sales targets.

The other expenses under the profit and loss account may be linked to the sales budget final data. For example, if the sale is 100 then the production budget can be 40 (COGS), the administrative budget can be 10% of sales, etc.

Administrative expenses may include expenses like rental, manpower, incentive, printing and all other multiple heads.

I will set a few examples here, however the rationale is just for example and not a rule. One can use a different logic and that is fine too.

Expense head	How to estimate/rationale
Rental cost	Basis headcount
Manpower cost	Basis percentage of COGS
COGS -production cost	Basis percentage of sales
Incentive	Basis percentage of sales
Marketing expenses	Basis percentage of sales
Accounts and finance department cost	Basis percentage of total manpower cost

Once you have base-year figures, the subsequent growth may not be in line with the proportionate growth of sales, but they will have a standalone rationale of growth as we start the mechanics of volume and economy of scale. For example, the expenses of manpower shall not double if the sales have gone up by 100%. I believe you now have got the logic behind the estimate and forecasting and a clear idea about the basics of planning and forecasting.

Pro forma statements, free cash flow and sensitivity analysis shall essentially enter into the zone of financial modelling, and the same has been explained in the next chapter. At this level, it is advisable to take the help of financial experts unless you are one of them.

Chapter 2.11

Financial Modelling

The basic purpose of putting this subject of financial modelling here is to give you a fair idea about what all goes into it. Financial modelling is also known as revenue modelling. This subject requires expertise, and thus, it  should be approached with caution. It is advisable to get it vetted with a financial modelling expert before presenting it to the investor.

Financial modelling essentially has the following sections:

- Assumptions and data drivers
- Income statement or profit and loss statement
- Balance sheet or net worth statement
- Cash flow statement or free cash flow to the firm
- Supporting schedules and groupings/workings
- Firm valuation and cost of capital
- Sensitivity analysis and what-if analysis
- Charts and graphs and other pictorial representation

Now, let's look at these heads in detail.

1. **Assumptions and data drivers:** All the financial modelling spreadsheet starts with an assumption and that, among others, usually has the historical data of the company. If the historical data is not available then we either take competitor data or industry reference data. Basis the past, you also assume the average receivable and payable cycles, working capital, etc.

2. **Income statement:** Here you will count all the heads of revenue to the extent possible. In case the segments represent at least 20% of overall revenue even in due course of an explicit period, then you should count each segment. You take out the cost of goods sold (COGS), other operating expenses and end up at EBITDA (earnings before interest, depreciation, taxes and amortization). Post this, take out depreciation, amortization, interest and taxes to reach at EAT (earnings after tax) or PAT.

3. **Balance sheet:** Until the income statement the path was simple, but a balance sheet involves some technicality. You need to be clear about the schedule of bank debt/interest, Account Receivable (AR)/Accounts Payable (AP) cycles, capital assets (property, plant and equipment), deferred revenue expenses, amortization schedule and a complete schedule of owner capital and long term/short term debts.

4. **Cash flow statement:** If you have the income statement and balance sheet ready, then the cash flow statement should not be a big issue as it is the collation of those statements but in a different format. A cash flow statement does not include non-cash items such as depreciation, etc. Here, anything that involves the inflow and outflow of cash will be counted irrespective of their position in the Profit And Loss Statement. For example, capital assets are not part of the income statement but that shall

be taken as cash outflow and not just the depreciation value for the period.

5. **Supporting documents and schedules:** This includes all the supporting documents related to industry research along with the sources based on which the assumptions have been made, including the growth rate, discount rate, ROI, receivable and payable cycle, etc. Other grouping and detailing include amortization schedule, clubbing of expenses to come to cost groups like manpower cost, establishment cost, finance cost and other administrative costs, etc.

6. **Enterprise value and cost of capital:** After we have the cash flow statement and projections ready for an explicit period, we apply for a valuation model known as discounted cash flow (DCF). In finance, DCF is the method of adding all future cash flows until infinite years at the present value. What could be the best rate to discount the future values shall depend upon the cost of capital. In general, we take the weightage average cost of capital (WACC). So, the firm value is the total of all cash flow till the business survives, and as per the concept of going concern, we take the life of the business as infinite unless there is something that suggests otherwise. The period can be finite in the case of businesses that have a limited cash flow period. For example, toll collection, airport right, etc.

7. **Sensitivity analysis:** Once we are ready with all pro forma statements of income, net worth and free cash flow and firm value, we do an analysis based on different scenarios of assumption and input. For example, we can use different data on the growth rate, discount rate, and COGS percentage and manpower productivity. This is done to convey to the investor or any other third party that the entrepreneur understands the nuances of

variation in his expectation and changing market fact. One can have a balanced view looking at the best and worst that can happen and take the appropriate decision.

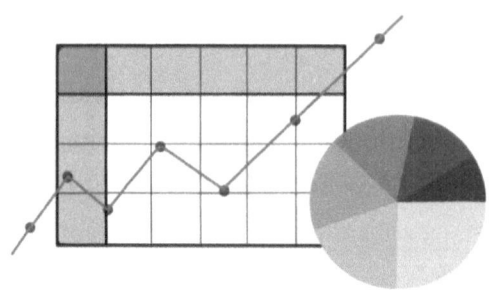

There are a few dos and don'ts while doing financial modelling that are as follows:

a. Do not make it too simple or too complex. In both cases, it will kill your plan and makes it less engaging.

b. Use colour scheme to differentiate between hardcoded numbers, input, formulas and output

c. Make an executive summary for brief understanding

d. Add flavour by adding pictorial representation with relevant diagrams and charts

e. Use similar format and fonts consistently

f. Mention the denomination of currency on every page

g. Write the name or logo on each spreadsheet

h. Make a separate cell for checking the totals and you may hide it once you are done with checking

i. Various possible ratios on the income statement and balance sheet should be included. For example, the gross margin ratio in the income statement and debt-equity ratio in the balance sheet. Any big changes, year-over-year (YOY) or quarter-on-quarter (QOQ), should be thoroughly checked and explained.

j. Your free cash flow statement deficit should match with the money being asked from investors. For example, if the YOY gives you a deficit of Rs. 5 crores, then if you do it MOM (month-on-month), the deficit shall rise in case you have contemplated the break-even during the year. If it is the year of fundraising, then you must make MOM details to check the highest cash-flow deficit.

k. Make different versions of modelling so that you do not lose the overall format and you could avoid the data from getting mixed up during iterations and Improvisations.

l. While doing sensitivity analysis, show the variables that are changing using different colours so that one could choose what is best suitable.

m. Discuss the model with someone who understands finances and ask for their feedback and then keep improving further

Chapter 2.12

Capital Budgeting

Capital budgeting is a standard process to define the mechanics of doing any capital expenditure (buying fixed assets) and evaluating the investment proposal available for a business at any given point of time.

Ideally, an organization would like to invest in all profitable projects, but due to the limited availability of capital and other resources, it has to choose between different projects/ investments.

For a better understanding of the capital budget, one should understand the meaning of capital expenditure first. Capital expenditure has the following three distinct features:

a. They have long term consequences on operational productivity.

b. They often involve a substantial outlay of funds or incurring of long-term liabilities.

c. It may be either difficult or very expensive to reverse these decisions.

Due to the above salient features, the capital budgeting exercise becomes important. The capital budgeting process can be divided into the following steps:

1. Identifying the possible investment option or opportunities

2. Making the investment proposal and comparison among them on various fronts

3. Choosing among the available option and decision making

4. Capital budgeting and fund apportionment

5. Implementation and performance review

The steps mentioned above are self-explanatory, and it is exactly like doing a small investment in household goods, like buying a refrigerator wherein you pass through all steps mentioned above. Starting from the need to buy a refrigerator to analyzing the cost and benefits of various brands and options available in the market to doing the cash outlay or taking a consumer loan, and then finally looking at the convenience and usage as compared to your expectations. These are the same steps followed when you decide to do any big cash outflow for the replacement of machinery or buying computers/plants or expansion, etc.

To assist the organization in selecting the best investment, there are various techniques available based on the comparison/correlation of cash inflows and outflow. These techniques are broadly categorized into two major segments basis the methodology of consideration of those time differential cash flows. Those two approaches are as follows:

A. **Non-discounting criteria/traditional approach:** In this technique, we do not calculate the time value of money, so no discounting is done even if the inflow/outflow happens after some time lag. Under this approach, the following two methods are prevalent:

1. **Accounting Rate of Return (ARR)**

   In this technique, the total net income of the investment is divided by the initial or average investment to derive the most profitable investment.

2. **Payback Period Method (PPM)**

   In this technique, the entity calculates the time required to earn the initial investment of the project or investment. The project or investment with the shortest duration is selected.

B. **Discounting criteria/modern approach:** In this technique, we calculate the time value of money and the present value of inflow/outflow which is happening at any future date other than the time of decision. Under this approach, the following method could be used:

1. **Net Present Value (NPV)**

   The net present value is calculated by taking the difference between the present value of cash inflows and the present value of cash outflows over some time. The investment with a positive NPV will be considered. In case there are multiple projects, the project with a higher NPV is more likely to be selected.

2. **Internal Rate of Return (IRR)**

   For NPV computation a discount rate is used. IRR is the rate at which the NPV becomes zero. The project with higher IRR is usually selected.

3. **Modified Internal Rate of Return (MIRR)**

   This is an improvement on the IRR method wherein it is assumed that project inflow is reinvested at the rate of the cost of capital than the project's own IRR. This is a more realistic approach in real life.

4. Profitability Index (PI)

Profitability Index is the ratio of the present value of future cash flows of the project to the initial investment required for the project.

Each approach and method comes with inherent advantages and disadvantages. An organization needs to use the best-suited technique to assist it in budgeting. It can also select different techniques for different investments depending upon the need of the hour and the longevity of the project.

In general, the business decision in a start-up business is done based on the IRR, which is similar to the concept of NPV. MIRR is good for knowing the true rate of return, but NPV takes the edge when we analyze mutually exclusive projects.

Irrespective of the method you use, you must have logical reasons for choosing that method and how the same is the most appropriate choice for your business.

After the stage of capital budgeting, you may also look at the various risks involved in the project. These risks can be standalone specific project risks or industry risks or market risks or global risks.

I suggest you keep in mind the behavioural biases and a few basic beliefs (people may call superstition) and be fully confident before you finally decide on the capital project.

Chapter 2.13

Raising Long-term Finance

As the word suggests, long-term finance includes all those sources of cash flows where the repayment is not really time-bound, such as common equity. On the other hand, short-term finance refers to  anything payable within one year of availing them. Therefore, any fund which is not payable within one year falls under the category of long-term finance. As logic, long-term finance is used to finance capital assets, such as expansion, modernization or diversification, etc.

Before we discuss how to raise long-term finance, let's first know the type of instruments which can be a source of long-term finance.

1. **Equity capital**: These are also known as ordinary shares capital and shareholders fund. These shareholders are the real owner of the company, and they have the right of dividend from the residual income of the company and these shares cannot be redeemed until the company survives. This is the permanent source of long-term finance.

2. **Preference capital**: The preference share capital is the second layer of the owner's fund. Preference capital is like the equity capital, but these involve the preferential right to receive fixed dividend, preferential right during liquidation as compared to ordinary/equity shares and these shares can be redeemed too if the terms so provide. Unlike equity shareholders, preference shareholders do not have any voting rights in the company unless their specific interest is being jeopardized.

3. **Debentures:** This is a debt certificate issued by the company as per the law (the Companies Act) and it bears a fixed interest and maturity period. These debenture holders also have the charge on the company's specific assets and are generally treated as secured creditors unless issued as unsecured.

4. **Long-term loans:** These are the loans issued and disbursed by banking and financial institutions, domestic or abroad and bear a fixed interest rate and repayment schedule. This may be secured or even unsecured depending upon the terms of the offer.

5. **Reserves and surplus**: The fund available inside the company is generally the extension of equity capital and consists of retained earnings of the business added with no cash expenditure like depreciation and other specific reserves. These are always available but are in limited supply.

Now the question is how to get these long-term finances. There could be multiple ways of looking at the availability and processes but, in general, the basic philosophy and methodology for sourcing the above instruments are as follows:

a. Venture capital and private equity

b. Initial Public Offering

c. Right issues and private placement

d. Banks and term loans

A. **Venture capital (VC) and private equity**: A start-up business concept that is not yet tried and tested in the market and is not eligible for raising long-term funds based on the options listed above, opt for venture capital. Venture Capital refers to the sum of money investors provide to start-ups with a promising business idea and practical future. The VC fund generally comes through equity capital or quasi-equity instruments like cumulative convertible preference shares (CCPS).

Earlier the Indian Development Financial Corporation (IDFC) and other national banks used to provide seed capital funds to grow the entrepreneurial skills and various small and medium businesses as a support mechanism than a profit-making exercise. However, SIDBI has the sole objective of supporting the SME sectors with various quasi-equity and other finance models.

The primary objective of VC funds is to invest in high-risk propositions with risk mitigation tools to maximize returns. They look for an exit after multiplying their investment in three to five years.

The VC fund is an important source of taking your start-up to the next level as it is a must-go avenue to raise the follow on round of funds. I have explained the process of getting VC and private equity investment in detail in the next chapter.

B. **Initial public offering (IPO)**: If we look into the corporate world and analyze the top 1000 companies around the globe and read about their history of growth, we will see that the biggest reason behind these companies becoming enormous and credible was the access to the capital market and stock exchange listing of their IPO.

IPO can be the biggest source of raising funds, creating value and wealth for promoters/investors and brand building. IPO also helps companies to lower their debt burden and increase profits, resulting in the retention of best talents through schemes like marketable ESOP or SARS (stock appreciation rights), etc. It is also an easy and tax-efficient tool for VC, angel investors and private equity investors to ensure their efficient and timely entry and exit.

In India along with the main board, we also have the SME exchange that provides emerging companies a viable option of raising equity capital and also paves the way for simpler listing on the main stock exchange at future date. India's premier stock exchanges namely NSE and BSE have created NSE Emerge and BSE SME respectively for emerging SMEs to raise capital to fund their growth. If you think IPO is for big companies, then think once more. If you are prepared and you have planned for IPO based on factors like due diligence parameters, compliance and disclosures, etc., your business too can opt for IPO.

In general, to become eligible for SME IPO, your business should be in existence for at least three years, with a profit-making trend and positive net worth. The promoters should have a sound track record and should be willing to comply with laws and disclose everything concerning their past and the future.

The other requirements shall be dealt with in great detail in the later chapter. There could be some additional requirements for your company, so it is better to check with an expert, while opting for the IPO mode.

Despite the simplicity, the IPO remains a complex process, therefore, you are advised to plan in advance and start the process by appointing your lead manager, who, in turn, will appoint merchant bankers, market makers, underwriter, registrar and bankers, etc. The lead manager also helps you prepare the offer documents that are filed and approved by the stock exchange and Registrar of Companies (ROC) before the public issue could be opened for subscription.

C. **Right issues and private placement**: Right issue means offering the right to the existing shareholders to subscribe to more shares at the issued price as decided by the company. So the rights and wealth of the existing shareholders are not diluted here but the company gets the required additional capital. In place of offering the right issue to the existing shareholders, the company may also issue shares to selected outsiders (maximum 200) chosen by the Board of Directors (private placement) subject to a special resolution of the company. The legal process of multiple filing with the ministry of corporate affairs has to be complied with for both the right issues and private placements. The minimum ticket size for private placement cannot be less than Rs. 20,000 worth of face value of securities. In the case of a private placement, a registered valuer, as defined in the Companies Act, must value the fair value of shares and these shares cannot be issued below the fair value. For completing and complying with the process of the right issue and private placement, you must hire a registered valuer professional.

D. **Banks and long-term loans**: The loan mentioned here should rather be called a project loan. The basic process for applying for a project loan is as follows:

1. You start with making a project report, which, among other details, has a financial plan of recouping the investment and the repayment of the borrowed sum.

2. Fill up the loan application form along with attachments, like project report, promoters' background, production plans, selling and manufacturing plans and all other economic and social considerations.

3. For better results (and if applicable), you must also get the technical and financial feasibility report done by a bank empanelled professional.

4. After the initial processing of the loan, you may be asked to supply some more information, and the appraisal of the project happens at the bank's end wherein the bank officer might visit the site.

5. Once satisfied with the norms of banking and lending, the bank issues the sanction letter indicating the terms and conditions of the sanction. Here you might like to negotiate a little on moratoriums for repayment and interest rates if the situation so warrants.

6. Once you have the loan sanction letter, the bank shall execute the loan agreement and create the mortgage by filing charge forms to the Registrar of Companies and/or as applicable to sub-registrar of the area where such security asset exists. The bank, depending upon the type of mortgage, may ask for the original title papers of property or registration of the mortgage.

7. After the completion of the above process, the disbursement of the loan amount is done either to you directly or through direct payment to your supplier.

8. Now the bank shall be monitoring the end-use of funds and operations through various reports periodically. You may also face a few audits from the bank's appointed auditors. The most prevalent among these audits are quarterly stock reporting and stock verification audits.

Banks and financial institutions generally consider the following aspects of the presented financial plan:

a. Debt equity ratio of maximum 1:1

b. Promoters' contribution to the maximum possible and at least 30%

c. Security assets are not in the negative area and at least cover 60% of the project fund as the remaining portion of required assets coverage comes in the form of primary mortgage of plant, land, building and inventory

d. Reasonableness of the estimate of capital cost/plant cost

e. Reasonableness of the estimate of working results and growth patterns reconciling with market norms

f. Adequacy of the rate of returns like ROI of the project and break-even point/payback time, etc.

g. Any signed-up LOI of buyer or supplier or technology partnership gives extra confidence to bankers

For raising long-term capital, you may also consider hiring an investment banker or an incubation advisory firm who can guide you through all these processes of raising long-term finance for different considerations like signing fees, fixed fees, success fees or sweat equity.

Venture Capital and Private Equity

A venture capitalist (VC) assumes the high risk and invests accordingly in the diversified portfolios of investee companies with the expectation of a higher degree of returns. These venture capitalists follow a rigorous diligence process to understand the complete risk be it financial or other business risks.

Like venture capital fund, the private equity investors again take the high risk in expectation of higher gain, but they come into the picture at a later stage when the revenue model has been proven and successfully run for some time. Private equity institutions/high net worth individual (HNI) are also  called growth fund because the primary reason for the funding at this stage is to grow and make it substantial before heading towards the public funding stage.

In both the VC and private equity (PE) funding, the fund is always managed by smart and intelligent professionals who run the business of investment and performance management and also help the investee companies to operate better.

In the last two decades, there has been a radical change in the investment philosophy, focused parameters and mutual dependence between investees and investors. VC/PE fund houses are no more being governed by few wealthy family offices but by more HNIs who invest in these funds for better return as compared to the stock market or conventional investments. So, these fund houses themselves are businesses, and they need to protect their own business too. A venture capital company generally has two layers of partners. The innermost owner layer is called LP (limited partners) who put in their fund in the VC fund, whereas, the other set of partners are called GP (general partners) who deploy and monitor the performance of the fund and take decisions related to the investment and suitable exit.

There are more than 100 active and large venture capital funds/ private equity firms, more than 1000 professional angel investors and 200 plus incubation and seed funds already operating in the Indian market alone. Besides, more investors are making their way to the Indian market because the Indian SME sectors have given many unicorns to the corporate world in recent times.

Other than a friendly environment, the government mechanisms also promote the SME sector by mandating priority lending, providing capital assistance schemes, etc. by SIDBI and NSDC/nationalized bank. There are few names you must know and those are ICICI venture fund, IFCI venture capital, Aditya Birla Private Equity, Softbank, Saif Partners, Sequoia Capital, Google venture fund, Microsoft Ventures, Tiger global and of course, you can Google for more.

What you need to check here is the investment philosophy of the fund and the criterion of their investment, which may be the nature of the business, size of funding or geographical boundaries. You must knock only those funds that are suitable for you. Applying at so many places without knowing the fund can be frustrating and, at times, your deal may get diluted and stale too. The benefits of getting VC funding are immense and among others, the most important is the benefit of having financial resources, without the burden of the payment of interest or scheduled repayment. For sure, you do lose equity ownership, but then for the VC, the future lies in the success of your business and then only it can get a decent exit and through this objective of the invested fund house, you are entirely taken care of on personal as well as the business front. They always look forward to better fund avenues, mergers, sale out, etc. and even use their network companies and influence to help your company on multiple levels.

Yes, it is a complicated and time-consuming process, and along with all other requisites, you have to be lucky enough to get the helping hand from a good VC/PE fund, who can accompany you on your growth path.

Generally, there is confusion between a VC and PE. The primary difference between a VC and PE is that a PE mostly buys 100% of the company that has a mature business, whereas a VC invests up to 50% and he/she focuses more on start-ups with potential growth.

So following advice, as applicable to you, must be considered on your path of raising funds from VC/PE:

1. **Quality of your pitch deck**: Irrespective of the VC fund, your pitch deck should be made appropriately using a plain and non-technical language that focuses on five critical aspects—problem, market, solution, team and competition. It should not be too long or too short. Venture capitalists sit in pitch presentations as their routine activity and so they can usually sniff out the nonsense in no time. Be upfront and true about your business's journey, challenges and plans. (Please read the other chapter on pitch book/IM for more details.)

2. **Decide if venture capital is right for you**: Venture capitalists expect to get eight to 10 times higher returns on their investment in less than five years. In addition to that, all the venture capital

funds have their category of funds which ranges from FMCG/ technology to HR, education, etc. Therefore, be sure that the VC fund, which you are approaching, has the allocable fund for your industry.

VC funds are not interested in linear and organic growth and will pressure you to manage the business to grow sales at some obnoxious rate. Not every company can achieve that kind of growth while maintaining brand value and product quality. If you do not plan on embracing that goal and the tactics to achieve it, do not waste your time talking to venture capital investors (unless a realistic business plan has been agreed upon) and rather go for other modes of funds, like family offices that see strategic importance in your start-up.

3. **Get the right introduction and attention:** A VC generally, if not always, relies on a trusted source of advisors and friends to send them transactions and potential leads. If someone outside that circle introduces you, odds are low that they will pay much attention. The most powerful introduction is from a mentor/early investor and secondly from founders of their investee companies, who have already earned their trust. The next best introduction would be from a client who is a genuine fan of your product and can credibly speak about you and your business. Never ask any investor to refer you to another investor, as investors selfishly guard their best deals for themselves and only share mediocre deals with even their best friends. You should always headline your introduction/first email with some worthy names, research or awards so that it beats the high competition in the mailbox of investors. The main objective here is to seek external and preferably an independent validation from someone regarding how promising and interesting your business is.

4. **Set promising but realistic expectations and milestones:** In general, in front of investors, we start talking big things and at times end up proposing unrealistic goals, which a well-groomed and educated investment professional understands really well and maybe better than you. You must be crystal clear on the immediate use of funds and create a clear milestone in the eyes of an investor basis which they could gauge and monitor your performance. The plan for investment/expenditure should be as precise as possible. For example, for a manpower budget, you must have clarity on aspects such as the talent required, their cost and deliverables and at least four quarters of milestone performance that can be measured easily.

5. **Showcase your product, service, or prototype:** It would be best if you could find an appropriate time to live showcase your product or service or working prototype. While you mention a lot about your business on paper and slides, it would be fantastic if a live product demo could be a part of your meeting. It will help the investor to give you immediate closure or rejection, which will be very helpful. However, choose a time slot that suits both the parties rather than imposing the display of your product. Create the curiosity first and then seek permission to live showcase.

6. **Keep the business plan ready:** Do not believe the myth that investors are high-flyers with a big wallet and have no time to read your business plan. The reality is that they have all the time to go through the assumptions, reasonability and research before they meet you. Post that, they have enough patience to hear you, analyze your behaviour and competency and then commence due diligence on your business before they finally open their wallet. The truth at the core of that myth is that investors may reject your business without reading your plan, but they will not

invest in it without reading the plan in detail. No business gets money without going through rigorous study and examination first (they call that "due diligence"), and the business plan is the active document for the due diligence. Your actual numbers should never be older than two weeks at maximum. (Please refer to the chapter on the business plan for more details.)

7. **Keep the meeting dialogue and not mono:** I have mentioned earlier, do not mistake to make your presentation as your speech, rather try all means to keep your presentation interactive, engaging and participative. You should be intelligent enough to pose quality questions and take feedback and suggestions from investors. You should be friendly enough to be asked tough questions and assertive enough to not become a 'Yes man' in front of investors. You should ideally divide the duration of the meeting to 50:50 between you and the investor. Just like you may not be 100% relevant to investors, they also might end up talking lots about their success stories and which may not be very useful to you, but I suggest you stay patient and appreciate their intelligence for better engagement.

8. **Big numbers and scalability:** It is true that a VC always looks for multiples of their investments than just high ROI, so unless you showcase a bigger picture by doing the market size research at a regional/global level and show scalability, it does not really make them interested. Your business should be logical at the present level and the need for funds should be showcased only for the next level of growth. After that, the business should sound scalable to a very big level (billions of dollars) at marginal cost increment. Your business plan should speak clearly about the sustainability, growth and scalability of your business.

So far we have focused on all those aspects that should be considered to impress a VC, get the appointment and have a productive and concluding meeting. Now, I want to list a few issues that may get you a wrong start or maybe straight rejection from a VC, so take care of the following facts:

a. The founder is not found to be an appropriate, expert and dynamic person to lead this type of business. As we say these days, they put money in people and not a business.

b. The market size is not big enough or scalability could be challenged.

c. Non-differentiator with a failed model or successful or big competitor

d. The business is under heavy lenses of regulators or strict rules for operating in the proposed geography.

e. The market place is already very crowded and there could be early technology disruption.

f. Too many founders/co-founders or investors/decision-makers, presidents, and mentors

g. A missing team member or leader of any vertical of business

h. The founder lacks vision and focus

i. Too small/too big/too early/too late

j. Competing/conflicting business with the portfolio company

k. Too big valuation and illogical terms for shareholding

l. Street smartness and too many tactics for raising funds

m. Licensing/ IP issues/ legality of concept

n. Difficult logistics and inappropriate market strategy

o. Any legal hassle or dispute among co-founders

p. Any dispute or negative words about key people or company

q. The unfavourable economic or political situation

r.   Too easy entry or substitution risk

The list mentioned above is not exhaustive but indicative, and one should work around these as reference points. If you could work around these negative references and have solid and logical response mechanisms (in case you face any of these), you are likely to win the race here.

Chapter 2.15

Hybrid Financing

Now we understand that long-term financing refers to equity and, to a large extent, few customized long-term debts. Both of the instruments have their own distinct characteristics which at times may or may not be suitable for a company.

For example, if one year down, you are set to achieve certain milestones and wonderful valuation and during the year, you have exhausted your cash and the same 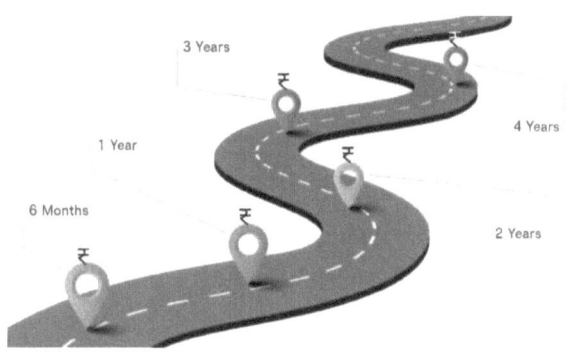 is becoming an impediment in achieving that milestone, you might like to take fund wherein you neither dilute your equity nor create an immediate repayment liability and so basically you want mixed features of both the debt and equity. These are few circumstances when the various instruments of hybrid finance take birth. So, basically, hybrid finance instruments facilitate you to take a long-term fund at a cheaper interest rate without diluting your equity at the present valuation. At the same time, a debt investor also looks for the upside of the risk of lending you in the hour of need.

Debt and equity are the two extreme points and in the middle lies the hybrid financing that offers the borrower company and investors the benefits of both the equity and debt.

There are several types of hybrid financing like preference capital, convertible debenture, warrants, innovative hybrids, and so on. Let's see those in details:

1. **Preference capital:** It carries a fixed rate of dividend which is payable at the discretion of directors when the company has a distributable surplus. The preference shareholders do not have voting rights in the company and depending upon other terms, their dividend could be accumulated year on year till paid out. The preference shares could be converted or redeemed at the option of the holder and he/she also has the option of time preferences as provided by law. The preference shareholders have the preferential right (as compared to equity shareholders) to claim their money in the event of winding up. The terms of preference shares may contain a call feature too whereby the issuing company enjoys the right to call the preference shares partially or fully.

2. **Convertible debenture:** It is a debenture that is convertible, partially or fully, into equity shares. The most notable feature of this debenture is that it promises a fixed income associated with debenture as well as a chance of capital gains associated with an equity share. The conversion premium/discount as well as the conversion period is always predefined.

3. **Warrant:** A warrant entitles the purchaser to buy a fixed number of ordinary shares at a particular price during a specified period. Warrants are issued along with debentures as sweeteners. Warrants give their holders the right to subscribe to a specified

number of equity shares of a company during a certain period at an exercise price.

Warrants and convertible debentures are commonly used instruments of financing around the world however in India, this started in the 80s and is now quite widespread.

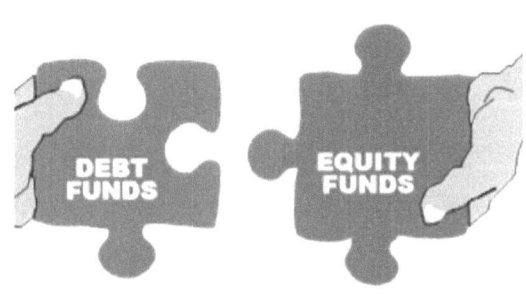

The reasons for the popularity of these hybrid instruments can be as follows:

1. **Cheaper cost of money:** The interest rates on debentures with a warrant or other call options are always lower as compared to the straight forward debt instruments like plain debentures. The option of conversion is always taken and valued as a transaction sweetener in the corporate world and investors' community.

2. **Arbitrage of equity premium:** Conversion prices in these options are always higher than the existing premium on equity. So these are also taken as an instrument to facilitate the issue of equity at a premium.

3. **Ease of getting finance:** In general, a new and fast-growing company having a good future prospect but not having a good present, finds it difficult to get equity investors due to the risk involved in uncertainty of success in novelty. However, the investor gets some respite owing to the certainty of interest payment and also the option to buy equity shares if the company does well. So, it is a win-win situation for both the company and the investor.

4. **Financial synergy:** A combination of debentures and options produces a financial synergy/risk synergy that enables an investor to pull a few plugs if the company does not go in a pre-defined direction. Therefore, the company ends up getting the fund at more favourable terms.

5. **Play of economics:** The hybrid instruments, unlike straight debt or equity instruments, provide a 'play' to investors wherein the investor could choose a different path later depending upon the opportunity, convenience and risk appetite. So, one may not be sure about the future of a company but still want to take a chance of getting investment multiple for small sacrifice on the interest rate.

6. **Cash on time:** Convertible notes are much faster than equity rounds. There are only two to three convertible investment agreements that outline the terms of the investment, valuation caps and discounts available. The promissory note explains the conversion and amount that the investor is investing. Even on the cost front, the convertibles rounds feature much better than equity rounds and cost maybe one-third of equity-based finance.

These days, the proliferation of creative and exotic versions of hybrids (interest rate, exchange rate, commodity index or other economic variables) is causing concern to many, and critics believe that hybrid is being taken as free lunch by many high-risk companies and is nothing but a supply-driven fad, invented by investment bankers for their own interest. But many wise economists and investors also believe this to be a useful capital market invention allowing great flexibility to both the parties. It is more like a compatibility check and risk-mitigating instrument before the parties go for an all-out partnership.

Chapter 2.16

Negotiation, Deal and Term Sheet

If you are contemplating this stage of talks with a VC fund or PE investor, then it very well indicates their positive inclination to participate in your business.

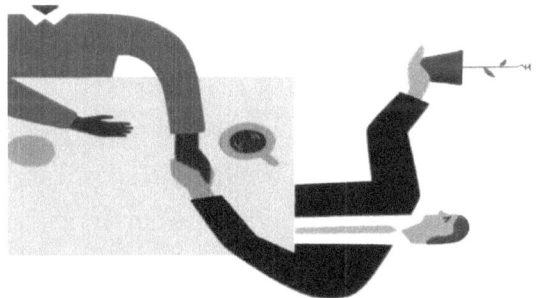

After a productive and concluding meeting with VC, the followings are immediate steps before you can expect the credit in your bank:

a. Few more emails and calls and document sharing

b. Presentation to all partners of the VC fund

c. Issuance, negotiation and closure of term sheet

d. Due diligence process

e. Drafting and finalization of various investor agreements like SHA and SPA, etc.

A VC deal can be valuable and transformative for an entrepreneur but at times the issues like enterprise valuation and equity dilution spoil the relation beyond repair even if the deal consummates. You must also focus on mentoring, strategic advice, network resources, and lobbying capital that a VC fund can offer along with money. It should be a win-win deal for both parties.

While on the one side, it is all about how much equity, control and rights a VC will have in return for its investment, on the other hand, these negotiations are more about selecting the right long-term partner and forging a relationship that can survive the lower performance, disappointments and unforeseen business conflicts and still targets to monetize the future milestones of success.

A VC deal brings considerable financial and non-financial resources and adds to the brand value of a start-up but only when the deal is done with the right intent and mindset of creating values, rather than just getting money and being covered in next day newspaper. Only with this line of thought, you could make a deal that takes full advantage of your strength, build a relationship of mutual trust and admiration and sign a contract that creates value (not just valuation). The aim should be to reach a level of understanding that ensures that each party will be appropriately rewarded for future success.

So, understand your leverage and its source properly and negotiate well on those. The leverages too should be used with caution, and it is better to be conservative and analytical about controlling power that lies with you after funding. Many times, entrepreneurs make a mistake by protecting equity dilution at the first funding and then dilute more when the business does not do well as anticipated. This makes the situation worse because the next investor now knows your desperation and takes you for a ride and, in the process, you lose your leverage forever. It is common to run out of cash before time, so you are suggested to give it a thought to probably dilute more in the first instance and raise some surplus fund or a prior arrangement of a need-based bridge loan or line of credit while negotiating the term sheet.

One of the factors that get disproportionate attention during the negotiation is the present valuation of the business rather than future value creation. The entrepreneur starts asserting the quantum of the funds that they need to procure and this mindset proves to be the biggest mistake in funding negotiations. This mindset is well understood by smart VCs, and they end up offering you the desired money but negotiate on the terms of control and reserved business items and additional board positions. As per rules of negotiation and if you are serious about the deal, you end up accepting those control rights in favour of investors and when a conflict or deadlock situation arises, you repent a lot with no recourse. Just to maximize the business valuation, you must not compromise with your control, self-respect, identity and independence. Financial consideration and valuations are very important but not at the cost of important non-financial considerations. Both sides are equally important.

You must also understand the origin of any condition put by the investor and play it accordingly to not only win the negotiation but also give extra comfort to the indicated area of concern. For examples,

- If a VC insists on enhancing the liquidation preference, this indicates the valuation proposed by the founders is too high.

- If a VC insists on board seats or other terms that define control, this shows that they are not confident about the management team and perhaps thinking of probable replacements.

- If a VC insists on non-conflict and non-competitors, this clearly indicates the trust issue with promoters and founders.

The next chapter will cover what all to be looked into term sheet and the legality of important clauses thereof when we deal with documentation and legal drafting.

One of the most sought after discussion that is negotiated in general is valuation. Valuation is important to both the parties equally and should definitely be given its due importance, but the issue with valuation is that it is a pure art though we base it on scientific calculations. There are many factors that affect the enterprise value. For example, the present market and economic condition, the promoter's career history, the lineage of an earlier start-up, capital intensity of the business, forecasted growth and CAGR of the industry and many more.

The company valuation and equity dilution are inversely proportional in nature. Generally, valuation is referred to as pre-money value (before investment) and dilution happens on the post-money valuation on a fully diluted basis.

To give you an example, if the business is worth (agreed pre-money valuation) Rs. 10 crores and the VC puts in Rs. 5 crores then, the post-money valuation shall be Rs. 15 crores. In this case, the ideal equity dilution here is 5/15 or 33.33%. The timing of the inflow and equity dilution may be post-investment or staggered or milestone-based.

You might face a situation wherein the VC may demand the founder's shares to have a vesting schedule, and this can be tricky if you do not negotiate this smartly. Ideally, do ask for a reasonable vesting credit for the already served term or simply do not accept it beyond a period. It is in the interest of the business and the VC that founders stay actively engaged and help to grow the business and that's why they insist on this. So if you satisfy the requirement through an undertaking of yourself and your key people (coupled with a well-drafted non-compete clause), the VC might forgo this requirement. It is better not to have such a vesting schedule because this may backfire on both parties due to the lack of ownership with promoters.

Another major issue that becomes tricky is the employee stock option size and deduction of this pool from pre or post-money shareholding. You should try to push it to post-money at least for all future hires, if not the existing key resources. If it stands as a deal-breaker for you, then in that case make an optimum size of stock option for a few key people ideally and just reduce the size of the option.

When you receive the term sheet, share it immediately with your lawyer and financial advisor to identify the top problems, and then decide the best step for moving forward and having a conversation with the investor to reach a common point. Ideally, you should finalize the term sheet within the first 72 hours from the time the investor sends it, and you should be ready to sign anytime thereafter unless there are some specific issues.

Finally, one of the non-cash items which you can negotiate well is the due diligence process, and though you cannot do away with this step, you can make it light on the business. You may just have a transparent conversation with the VC and ask the concerns and try to resolve and talk them out. If the due diligence becomes detailed, then it will consume a lot of time and energy at both ends, and it can even jeopardize the deal overall. The due diligence may happen through a third-party audit/consulting firm, so you may also request a defined timeline of the closure of process and limited diligence too may be agreed upon. You must be clear about the cost of an attorney and due diligence. You should agree only for a minimum possible fee/capped fee, payable only on the closure of the transaction and not before that.

The terms sheet lists the understanding you have with investing partners. It lists the major understanding you may have arrived at and the basis on which substantive agreement will be executed. When you enter into any discussion and negotiation with an investor, you must sign off an investor meeting with a definitive summary document or minutes of the meeting, mentioning the point which has already been agreed upon. This may act as a record of resolved points that either of you may need to go back and recall. This shall save time and energy in subsequent meetings and give a good base of mutual consensus to talk next points

The term sheet, in reference to SHA, SSA and SPA, includes the points which have been agreed for different clauses of such agreements. If the term sheet has been comprehensibly prepared and signed, subsequent documentation will be faster as the point of negotiations has already been covered and hence finalization of substantive agreements like SHA, SSA and SPA will be smoother.

When you discuss the legal implications of various terms of legal agreements including that of the term sheet, you must hire the best and seasoned attorney to advise you on the legality of the deal and an equally good investment banker/financial advisor who can advise you on the ideal valuation for your business and strategic fixes during the making of a deal.

Chapter 2.17

Due Diligence Review

Due Diligence is an important milestone in the process of raising long-term finance from VC or any other institutional investor. The investor or, on their behalf, a third-party assurance advisory firm conducts this diligence exercise to confirm the accuracy of claims made by a business and entrepreneur. This may cover topics like the financial statement, assets upkeep or stocks check or walkthrough on operation process, employee satisfaction survey, checking of the authenticity of receivables, intellectual property rights and many more as per specific requirement and operating standards of the fund house.

The length and type of due diligence totally depend upon the agreement between the parties and the level of comfort an investor is looking for in any specific area of operations and also the key revenue drivers. There could be various types of due diligence reviews, but the two major reviews that generally occur are as follows:

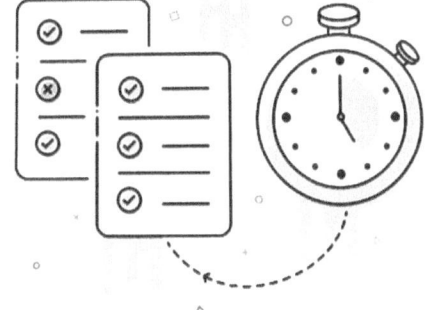

a. Financial due diligence

b. Legal and secretarial due diligence

Essentially, you may face the investors themselves through their in-house accountants, attorneys, financial officer and IT controller and then a third-party assurance firm appointed by them. Finally, there could be some valuation consultants and merchant bankers for the fair valuation of specific assets owned by the company and that drive the value of the business.

The due diligence reviews are in the nature of management audit and to some extent an investigation. The process commences simply by sharing the standard list of information required and then post sharing the original list, a possible follow-up list or visit to company premises or commencement of any survey process. You should expect the due diligence to be a process of approximately two to four weeks unless there is information holding at your end or the audit team sniffs some kind of fraudulent practices. You should be very upfront on the sharing of information in pre-defined formats so that the interpretation becomes faster as well as accurate. You should also disclose all related party transactions and any other exceptional transaction, which you think could put you in trouble, with a possible explanation. However, you might like to address these with investors separately too. Coming with these disclosures upfront might help you to not get questioned on integrity and avoid possible confrontation with third-party auditors or simply take those out of the diligence list if so agreed by the investors.

Now let's see the two major due diligence in detail.

1. Financial due diligence

The objective of this diligence is to not only check the present business valuation and cash flows but also the future maintainable earnings and scalability claims of business. Unlike an audit exercise, the auditors are governed by the interest of investors and the scope of work assigned to them. These auditors are more interested in the cause and effect, normalization of present operating margins and rationalization of a forecast rather than the true and fair views. The list of information and topics that are covered in the financial due diligence review (DDR) are as follows:

a. Standard operating procedures or accounting manual and employee handbook that clarify the company policy on all possible accounting and administrative items

b. Company identity details with all possible registrations like the certificate of incorporation, MOA, AOA, trademark and other IPR copies, etc.

c. Copy of PAN, TAN, registration certificates of VAT, service tax, GST, Excise, PF, ESIC, shop, and establishments for all premises used, IEC code, and any other registration certificate as applicable to the company

d. Business presentation and financial plan

e. The past three years audited financial (lesser if applicable) and respective tax returns

f. List of all major clients and billing

g. List of all major suppliers and purchases

h. Copy of one-year internal audit reports if any

i. List of all associated companies, related party buyers/suppliers for all founder and key management people

j. Employee's data along with qualification, tenure, remuneration and other employee benefits

k. Details regarding the working space, leasing and lock-in, etc. for all occupied premises that are the head office, registered office, corporate office and other sales offices

l. List of all consultants (legal, financial and others) and their retainer or other fees paid to them for at least one year

m. Details of marketing and promotional expenses

n. Details of technology or other assets built or purchased along with the schedule of amortization

o. Bank statements, loan repayment schedules, sanction letters of any working capital loan, credit cards, etc.

p. Advance tax, TDS, indirect tax workings, payment *challans* and returns copy for one to two year

q. Any tax dispute or letter of intimation or scrutiny from direct or indirect tax departments

r. Advances received from debtors or advances paid to creditors

s. List of extraordinary and prior period transactions

2. Legal due diligence

The objective of legal due diligence is to check the legal and secretarial hygiene, legal hindrances in the long-term sustenance as a going concern, risk of future litigation and provisioning for such contingent legal liabilities in books of accounts and forecasted financials.

In general, the following points get covered in the legal due diligence information list (a few points might sound duplicated but the financial and legal are different people and so you will have to supply to both):

a. Copy of registration of the company along with MOA/AOA and copy of all tax registrations

b. List of all related party organization and entities for all the founders and Key Managerial Persons (KMP)

c. List of shareholders and their participation also known as the CAP table

d. Personal KYC details of all substantial shareholders

e. All the registers maintained under applicable laws like the Companies Act. For example, register of members, register of charges, etc.

f. Copy of earlier signed shareholder agreement and other relevant undertakings and terms of holdings

g. Stock option plan and details of KMP

h. Copies of all share certificates and share transfers

i. Minutes book of companies for both the board of director and shareholder meetings

j. Major agreements of buyers and sellers and information of vendor empanelment agreements

k. Title documents for any real estate

l. Mortgage papers for the charge on any fixed assets

m. Loan sanction letters and repayments schedules

n. Statutory and internal auditors report if any

o. Copies of application of IPR and IPR grants as on date and details of objection filed with the registrar if any

p. Copies of all employment agreements (at least KMP) and other indemnities signed for or against

q. Any legal dispute of any nature being contested by the company for or against and all the documents related to such dispute

r. Tax inquiry and investigation for all periods and the final assessment order for the last three years

s. Copy of general liability insurance and all other applicable insurances like a key man or medical or assets general insurance (as applicable)

t. Broker and franchisee agreement if applicable

u. Contracts with related parties if any

v. Any joint venture, MOU, partnership, non-compete or non-conflict agreement

w. Any other relevant agreement or communication is done for or against the company irrespective of financial implication

Over and above, these documents related to financial or legal due diligence, depending upon your business nature, may be subject to diligence audit for IT and Software, environmental clearances, carbon footprints, employee happiness, customer satisfaction survey, quality audits and many more. What all diligence may happen is totally dependent upon the term sheet negotiation and waiver obtained in this regard. Irrespective of how complex and frustrating the process is, you have to pass through it. Besides, irrespective of the outcome of such DDR, the process will help you to think beyond your daily works and make the company's standards and system more robust and future-ready. A successful due diligence review does not only bring you investment but gives you satisfaction with regard to your house being in order. Many people have started passing through a pre-DDR these days, and you too might opt for the same if the circumstances and your financial position allow so.

Chapter 2.18

Enterprise Valuation

The valuation of a business is an art based on science. Though there are various approaches, methods and guidelines around valuation, there is no legal mandate as to how to value a business and what is best suitable for a particular buyer or a seller. The same company may be of different value for the  different buyers at different valuation dates. Many of the international accounting standards and international valuation standards, which talk about the enterprise valuation, are more of recommendatory rather than mandatory.

While purchasers or investors seek to acquire equity at the minimum possible price and favourable terms for better control on the company, at the same time, an entrepreneur aims at maximizing the price and securing optimal independence and control going forward. Despite this basic difference in thought, there is one powerful common point that they both want the deal to happen and so reaching a fair value, which is acceptable to both, is the common goal. While valuation and economic value are of immense importance, for reaching a fair value, the entrepreneur should also value the non-financial compensation. I must quote here the legendary Warren Buffett differentiating the price and value. He says, *"Price is what you pay and value is what you get. So value can be monetary and non-monetary too."*

There could be multiple methods of valuation suggested by professionals around the world basis their experience and the prevailing market trends, but in the end, the most appropriate fair value is the transaction value on which both the buyer and seller sign off the deal.

The definition of the fair value indicated everywhere including the IAS, IFRS and IVS revolves around three factors:

a. Fixed transaction date

b. Transaction price, which is agreed between the buyer and seller for exchanging hands

c. In an orderly transaction, which means a free flow market (where there are a number of buyers and sellers), and without any obligations on either of the parties

To an entrepreneur, selling the business typically means parting with something extremely valuable. It may sound logical to grow the business and sell it at an appropriate price but this is also a very emotional decision for an owner. Though you may have pre-worked the calculation of business value basis one or other scientific methodology under the advisement of your financial advisor, you are suggested to keep the following points in mind:

a. Have good information about the buyer/investor and their perspective on the deal or maybe a few weak spots if possible

b. Have faith in your business and have the mindset that this is not the only option you have and it is ok to walk away too

c. Be clear on the bottom number beyond which you will not go down. You may consider making the offer rather than hearing the offer but it depends on a specific situation. It is absolutely okay to make an offer to investors.

d. Avoid conceding on other terms like control and reserved business if the business valuation needs to be discounted beyond your expectation

e. You must know the difference between business valuation for financial investment and strategic investment. Financial investment is only financial contribution while strategic investment is a combination of both monetary and non-monetary thrust to business.

f. A valuation that is ideal and not practical and that cannot be closed is a bad valuation. Try to conclude the valuation as soon as possible and keep it in writing in one or another form within 24 hours of such a conclusion and do not wait for all legal drafting to get completed.

Now, let's get into a few technical processes of the valuation of a business. As mentioned earlier, there could be many methods of valuation but the best suitable needs to be taken up for discussion and closure..

There are several methods and techniques used for valuation, however, these methodologies fall under three basic approaches of valuation:

- Income Approach
- Market Approach
- Cost Approach

Income Approach: This is a valuation approach that converts all the future maintainable amounts (e.g., cash flows or income and expenses) to a single current amount (i.e., discounted or capitalized). This approach essentially involves discounting future amounts to their present value basis the current market expectation (discount rate). The income approach is appropriate in instances where:

a. The asset does not have any market comparable or comparable transaction

b. The asset has fewer relevant market comparable

c. The asset is an income-producing asset for which the future cash flows are available and can reasonably be projected

The common valuation methods under the income approach are:

- Discounted Cash Flow (DCF)

- Relief from Royalty (RFR)

- Multi-Period Excess Earnings Method (MEEM)

- With and Without Method (WWM)

- Option Pricing Model

Market Approach: This valuation approach uses prices and other relevant information generated by similar market transactions involving identical or comparable assets, liabilities or a group of assets and liabilities or a business overall or a single cash-generating unit (CGU) of big business.

Market Approach is appropriate in instances where:

a. The asset to be valued or a comparable or identical asset is traded in the active market

b. There is a recent orderly transaction in the asset to be valued

c. There are recent comparable orderly transactions in an identical or comparable asset(s) and information for the same is available and reliable

The common valuation methods under the Market Approach are

- Market Price Method

- Comparable Companies Multiple (CCM)

- Comparable Transaction Multiple (CTM)

Cost Approach: Cost approach is a valuation approach that reflects the amount that would be required currently to replace the service or production capacity of an asset (often referred to as current replacement cost). This approach is of least importance as these are generally used in the liquidation process.

The common valuation methods under the Cost Approach are:

a. Replacement Cost Method

b. Reproduction Cost Method

c. Summation Method

We learned the basic categorization of business valuation, but there are specific situations like the one in case of a start-up where the historic data is not available or revenue is yet to commence. In early start-ups or the SME sector, in more than 90% of cases the following methods (in order of priority) are prevalent:

- **Comparable multiple methods (Market Approach):** The market multiples are analyzed basis the deal flowing in the market and anything can be made the key factor. For example, it could be sales or EBIDTA or EBIT or PAT multiplied by applicable multiple factors.

- **Discounted cash flow (DCF under Income Approach):** The cash flow projection could be rationalized and normalized and after that, the DCF valuation is done.

- Specific methods like the VC method, Berkus Method, Risk Factor Summation, etc. which are a mix of cash flow capitalization, market sentiments/norms and risk premium/ROI expected by the investor.

In short, if your business falls under a specific category wherein the market multiple has been established, that will be the number one priority and in absence thereof the DCF method is generally followed. This valuation may further be balanced out through a specific method applicable to you depending nature and size of your business.

It is good to know in advance the methodology best suitable in your case and which is also acceptable to your buyer/investor. After that, create a list of exceptions for a higher valuation by collating all possible data and tables of extraordinary and non-recurring costs, which may have been put in the cash flow statement and if removed, you may push the normalized revenue upward. In the case of the market multiple methods too, you could seek a premium multiplier basis few new factors applicable to your business. For example, the management team and awards won by your business in the recent past.

Moreover, the other point of creating an upward valuation could be the consideration for the valuation of the intangible property of the company. This may include the brand name, goodwill and other registered or registrable intellectual property rights.

Collating these extraordinary items with respective details helps you to either push the valuation upward or at least helps you to negotiate other terms of investments more confidently.

Chapter 2.19

Drafting of Legal Agreements (SHA, SSA and SPA)

Be it starting a business with co-founders or on-boarding a technology or financial partner or signing an agreement with an investor, a legal agreement and the clauses therein are of immense importance as these decide how the future course of business shall be undertaken together. These documents are the foundation of your future relationship with your co-founder, equity partners and investors. Since the documents decide the fate of your business, they deserve some deeper understanding.

Before we move on to define the importance of legal agreements, let's understand the terms that are used in common parlance. SHA stands for Share Holder Agreement; SSA means Share Subscription Agreement (SSA) and SPA means Share Purchase Agreement (SPA).

Although the purpose of these documents is almost similar, each of these is executed at different stages of investment in a start-up company.

Now let's understand the purpose of the different documents mentioned above. I will discuss these documents in the same order as they occur at different stages of your business.

Share Holder Agreement (SHA)

This document is executed at the inception stage of your business. This document is basically made to define the relationship among the persons who join hands to start a business and incorporate a limited liability company. It must be executed (terms agreed and the document signed) before any step is taken towards initiating the business venture. Depending upon the stage, the document can be called a pre-incorporation agreement if it is signed before the incorporation of the business and post-incorporation agreement if it is signed after the incorporation. It may also be called a shareholder agreement. The following are the points which must be included in the SHA:

- Parties in an SHA are all those people who join the business as equity owners

- The ownership ratio has to be decided beforehand, and it reflects in filing with the Registrar of Companies

- Amount to be invested by each party over and above share subscription

- Avoid two captains in one ship. You may agree for flexibility in controls, but the binding management structure has to be decided beforehand.

- The lock-in period of transfer of shares (ownership) by the promoters. Seed fund investors and even VC fund investors will be keen to know the continuing obligations of promoters.

There are other critical terms for SHA that are similar to SSA and SPA. These terms are discussed in the section 'Points Common to SHA, SSA and SPA'.

Share Subscription Agreement (SSA)

As the name suggests, this agreement is executed when an investor or strategic partner joins a running company with an existing business. This agreement is generally executed at the funding stage. Unlike SHA where all parties have similar interests, the SSA has two sets of parties. On one side there are founders/promoters and on the other side, the investors. Promoters have the main interest in funds, which they need to scale up the business, whereas investors have an interest in increasing the valuation of their investment. From the business control perspective, promoters will have an interest in maintaining the operational autonomy, and investors will have an interest in the wise use of their funds, protection against the dilution of their acquired ownership and obligation of the promoters towards business continuity.

To define the terms of understanding to maintain a balance between such varied interests following terms are important:

- The final valuation of the business and methodology adopted now and all future incidences of shareholding transactions

- Once the valuation has been completed and the same has been agreed upon by the investor, the next point that needs to be agreed upon is the quantum of the investment amount.

- The investor may agree for lump sum investment or they may insist on the milestone-based investment. In cases of staggered funding, the investors are allotted partly paid-up share and the subsequent calls are made as per the schedule agreed upon.

- The kinds of shares to be issued and agreement on preferential treatment norms be it dividend or exit right. In general, either equity or preference shares are issued that have different rights and liabilities or maybe hybrid instruments like convertible preference shares, which are in fashion these days.

▪ Directorship and board position are generally mentioned in SSA and is one of the negotiated terms because it gives control to investors and takes away the autonomy of the promoters. You must ensure that you have maximum representation on the board of the company. The lesser the number of directors appointed by investors, the better it is for you.

▪ The main purpose of an investor for investing in a start-up is to get an exit at a higher value. Sometimes an investor may insist on a definitive timeline on the expiry of which he/she will be provided the option to exit and the minimum value of such exit. This is called redemption right. Redemption rights may be agreed upon but, at the same time, they should not be made a liability of the founder.

▪ Unlike SHA, in the case of SSA, the investor will become part of a running company with operational history. Many times, these investors look for representation, indemnity and warranties from the promoter against the past liabilities if any which may come on company and them too, as part of the company. Hence all the details, documents and representations that have been relied upon by the investor must be stated in the SSA so that in case of allegations of misstatement, the same could be referred to.

▪ Protective provisions or a restricted business or reserved business is again one of the most contested topics, wherein few transactions are agreed to be executed only with prior approval of investors. This empowers the investors but curtails the independence of an entrepreneur. The examples of such protective provisions are as follows:

  ◆ Repurchase, redeem, buy back or otherwise acquire any shares of the company

  ◆ Declare or pay any dividend

- Issue indebtedness in excess of a certain sum

- Acquire any equity interest in any entity or acquire material assets of any

- Any amendment to the Company's Articles of Association, Memorandum of Association or similar documents

- Create any new class of shares or securities

- Liquidate, dissolve or wind-up the operations of the company

- Sell material assets that exceed a certain limit

- Make any material change like the company's business

- Issue additional/new shares of any nature

- Merger, consolidation, or substantial sale of assets

- Dilute the voting rights of investors

- Any strategic/financial/other alliance

- Change in the name of the company

- Any change in the board structure

- Any change in the founder's remuneration

The shorter the list of reserved business, the better it is for founders and entrepreneurs.

The Common Points in SHA and SSA

There are a few clauses that are common between SHA and SSA. These clauses control the right to deal in the shares of the company and similar incidental and auxiliary rights. Some of the important clauses under this category are as follows:

Lock-in period: The lock-in period ranges from three to five years. In common understanding, it is assumed that a business generally takes three years to get stable. And hence, it is required that promoters stay together for at least three years, therefore, this obligation/restriction is mentioned both in SHA and SSA. Under this condition, it is stated that promoters cannot transfer their shares within the prescribed lock-in period.

Right of first refusal: This clause provides that if any shareholder wishes to transfer their shares, then they shall first offer those shares to the existing shareholders, and the existing shareholders can purchase those shares in their exiting shareholding ratio. It protects the existing shareholders from the dilution of both their ownership percentage and the value of their shares. If the lock-in period is either not applicable or has expired, none of these clauses restrict a shareholder from selling his/her shares, rather it protects the continuing shareholders against unfriendly strangers entering the business.

Tag-along right: One of the major purposes of a start-up company is value creation. Value creation happens with the efforts of all, be a promoter (professional or technical effort) or investor (financial effort), and hence the benefit of value creation should also be distributed proportionately. This clause ensures the same. It provides that if any shareholder is willing to sell his/her shares, every other shareholder shall have the right to participate in the sale process in their shareholding ratio. The shareholder will have both rights available—right of first refusal and tag-along right. Depending on his/her choice, he/she can choose either of them. This clause generally protects the rights of minority shareholders.

Drag along right: This clause protects the interest of the person with the majority shareholding. It provides that in case the majority of shareholders want to sell all of their shares to any entity, then they can drag other shareholders with them. The only condition that is included in this clause is that shares of other minority shareholders shall not be sold on terms that are less favourable than terms on which the majority shareholder is transferring their shares.

Information right: As a shareholder, one has the right to seek certain information from the company as the same has been provided under the Companies Act, 2013. However, those rights are quite general and may not give specific insights into the business operations of the company that may answer the curiosity of an investor. Through the rights under this clause, an investor will be able to ensure that he/she is supplied with the periodical financial data sufficient to assess the company's financial position.

Restrictive covenants of promoter: A promoter will be able to successfully lead a business only when he/she will devote full time and energy to the business. To ensure this, the following restrictive covenants are necessary:

- Restriction on starting a separate venture whether conflicting or not
- Restriction on taking up any full-time employment or any other engagement
- Non-compete clause
- Restriction on any investment in any other entity

Share Purchase Agreement (SPA)

This document is generally executed when a promoter sells all or a substantial part of ownership in the company. Since the transaction covered by SPA is different from the SHA or SSA, the clauses of the SPA are also different. SHA and SSA are for investment in the company, whereas the SPA is for the exit of the promoter(s). As the

nature of the transaction has changed, we need to change the reference name of the parties too. In SPA, there are two parties: the seller (who is selling his shares) and the purchaser (who is purchasing the shares).

Terms of sale purchase: SPA has to provide for a percentage of ownership being acquired and agreed consideration for acquisition.

Representations and warranties by the seller: As is the case in SSA, the purchaser will purchase the shares of a running company with operational history. The purchaser will rely on details, documents and representations as made to them by the seller/promoter. Although the purchaser will carry on their due diligence, there may be many details that cannot be verified immediately. At the same time, there could be an allegation in the future, on the promoter that they did not disclose any particular detail which may have financial implications, and, as the result, the purchaser took an uninformed decision. Therefore, this clause is important for the purchaser and seller both to avoid any contingency and protect their bona fide right and intention.

Indemnity by seller/promoter in favour of purchaser: For a similar reason as stated in the case of SHA, indemnity is an important clause in the case of SPA too.

Restrictive covenants on promoter: It is important for the purchaser that the seller/promoter agrees that they will not

- Join any other entity having business similar to or competing with business of the company of which shares are being sold

- Carry business similar to or competing with the business of the company

- Hire the employees of the company or entice them to join any other company or entity

- Solicit any business with the existing client of the company or divert any order of the company for an agreed period. Generally, the agreed period varies from three years to five years.

Another particularly important point that should be categorically made clear is the timeframe of such restriction and also the territorial limits.

Chapter 2.20

Employee Stock Option

An employee stock option plan also known as the stock option is one of the best tools for employee incentive and retention in a start-up or SME. This tool helps employees to not only get benefits but also get proportionate ownership. As a result, the employee's interests get aligned with the company's performance through optimal manpower productivity.

Under the Employee Stock Option Plan (ESOP), the employer (generally a limited liability company) grants its employees an option to buy a certain number of shares at a predefined price, which is usually lower than the market price. ESOPs in India are governed by the Companies Act and specified rules, Income Tax Act and in case of a listed company by the SEBI norms. I am focusing more on the ESOP mechanism in start-ups and small companies and not in a big-listed company. There are three important stages in the allotment of shares under the ESOP scheme:

Grant: The grant of an ESOP refers to the offer made by the company by issuing the 'Letter of Grant' informing the concerned employees about their eligibility to avail benefits under the scheme.

Vesting: It is the process that gives an employee the right to own shares in his company over a period of time. Generally, this occurs after 12 months of grant, but this period can vary as per other norms.

Exercise: After the stage of vesting, the employees can exercise the right to get the shares allotted to them as per the letter of grant. Such a request for allotment made to a company is called exercising the option.

For introducing the ESOP in any company, the ESOP is drafted and approved by the Board of Directors (along with names and entitlement of specified employees) and then in a general meeting of the shareholders of the company. The ordinary resolution (unlisted private company) or special resolution (unlisted public company) so approved in general meeting then gets filed with the Registrar of Companies.

Basis the shareholder resolution, the offer of a grant can be distributed to the concerned employees and such a letter must contain all the terms and conditions of allotment like vesting period, exercise price and lock-in if any.

These ESOPs are subject to income tax, and taxes are levied at two instances as discussed below:

- On the date of exercise, the amount of gain, which is the difference between fair market value (FMV) and the exercise price of shares, is taken as perquisite and taxed under the head salary.

- On the date of sale of such shares by employees, the difference between the sale prices and FMV is taxed as a capital gain. It depends upon the holding period for this being a short-term or long-term capital gain.

In my experience, to make it a tax-efficient tool, the employees generally do not exercise the option until the event of funding (liquidation event) in a company, wherein they could get the opportunity to sell and liquidate their shares. Otherwise, the shares of start-ups that are not saleable in the market bring unnecessary tax burden at the time of exercise and cash loss situation occurs. In the recent budget, the flexibility of postponing such taxes for five years has been introduced, which is subject to compliance with certain other terms and conditions.

Now, the question arises to who all it can be issued and what are the legal provisions in this regard?

Section 62(1) (b) of the Companies Act 2013 and Rule 12 of the Companies (Share Capital and Debentures) Rules, 2014, together provide for the provision of ESOP.

As per the section and rules mentioned above, the ESOP can be issued to

1. Any permanent employee of the company who has been working in India or outside India or of a holding company of the company

2. Any director of the company, excluding an independent director, who has been working in India or outside India or of a holding company of the company

Provided, the following are excluded:

1. An employee who is a promoter or a person belonging to the promoter group

2. A director, who either himself or through his relative or body corporate, directly or indirectly, holds more than 10% of the outstanding equity shares of the company

Keep the following points in mind while drafting the ESOP and issuing the letter of grant and share allotment:

1. There should be a minimum 12-month gap between granting and vesting of shares

2. An employee shall not have any right of a shareholder until the option has been exercised and shares have been allotted

3. The option granted under the ESOP scheme is non-transferable

4. Approval from shareholders shall be sought to grant shares to the employees of a subsidiary or holding company

5. In case of resignation or termination of employment during the grant period and before vesting, the option shall cease, but if there is permanent disability or death, the option grant shall stand vested.

6. The fair market value of shares must be certified by a registered valuer registered with IBBI as defined under section 247 of the Companies Act 2013.

The sweat equity shares are different than ESOP and those sweat equities are issued as per rule 8 of the Companies (Share Capital and Debentures) Rules, 2014 and have the following salient features:

1. A company shall not issue sweat equity shares to its directors or employees at a discount or for consideration other than cash, for providing know-how or making available rights in the nature of intellectual property rights or value additions, unless the issue

is authorized by a special resolution passed by the company in general meeting.

2. The sweat equity shares issued to directors or employees shall be locked-in/non-transferable for three years from the date of allotment. The fact that the share certificates are under lock-in and the period of lock-in shall be stamped in bold or mentioned in any other prominent manner on the share certificate issued to them.

3. The company shall not issue sweat equity shares for more than 15% of the existing paid-up equity share capital in a year or shares of the issue value of Rs. 5 crores, whichever is higher. Total sweat equity shares in the company shall not exceed 25% of the paid-up equity capital of the company at any time. However, with the recent amendment in 2020, the start-up could issue sweat equity up to 50% of the paid-up capital.

4. The amount of sweat equity shares issued shall be treated as part of managerial remuneration for sections 197 and 198 of the Act, if the following conditions are fulfilled, namely

   a. The sweat equity shares are issued to any director or manager

   b. They are issued for consideration other than cash, which does not take the form of an asset that can be carried to the balance sheet of the company in accordance with the applicable accounting standards.

5. The fair market value of shares must be certified by a registered valuer with IBBI as defined under section 247 of the Companies Act 2013.

Many of the provisions applicable to ESOP and SWEAT are similar except for the fact that sweat equity may be misused for tax evasion hence, it follows under stricter norms.

One must be clear about the list of people who will be issued sweat and those who will be covered under ESOP. And before deciding on the specific provisions related to the same, it is important to consult a professional. Taxations are nearly the same for both sweat and ESOP.

There are many other similar arrangements developed in the recent times of issuing the option shares to mentors, employees, directors, advisors and consultants wherein either equity subscription option or share value appreciation right could be awarded to them in place of cash remuneration. These are popular as SARs, phantom stocks, stock purchase plan, etc.

The existing legal framework in India is not very clear on phantom stocks and advisor shares, etc. but these concepts have become even more relevant in this COVID-19 era wherein the uncertainty of business is forcing the postponement of cash pay-outs and more roles of equity derivatives. The company is at liberty to plan the scheme of grant and allotment of these rights/options within four corners of laws.

Section 3

BEYOND 1000 DAYS

Chapter 3.1

Strategic Management

Many of us consider the word 'strategic management' just as camouflage for talking big and wishful. As we understand that the primary questions concerning the "what", "why"  and "how" have already been taken care of by the founder, and the founder has a clear vision of what to do, the next level question is what role does strategic management play in making and shaping of this vision?

This chapter is dedicated to defining the pivotal role a tool like strategic management plays in the overall growth and stability of a business.

I must state a Japanese proverb here which says, *"Vision without action is daydream but action without vision is a nightmare."*

Strategic management is nothing but planning for both predictable as well as unpredictable future contingencies. It is applicable to both small as well as large organizations as even the smallest organization faces multiple challenges and competition, and by formulating and implementing suitable strategies, these organizations can attain sustainable growth. Strategic management is a way in which an entrepreneur sets the objectives and cautiously proceeds towards attaining them. It helps to set the right direction for a business at any given point in time.

Strategic management is a continuous process that evaluates and controls the business environment and then re-evaluates the existing strategies and processes on a regular basis to determine how these have been implemented and what more changes may be needed to make those more suitable.

A small business is also affected by changing economic and other macro market scenarios that are external in nature and cannot be controlled by the mere one-sided hard-working manpower and well-groomed management. In those changing scenarios, the small business needs guidance on the adaptation of changes and dynamic planning. Strategic management practices give that backbone to small businesses in bad days, and if the specific process and characteristics of business have been counted and considered in making those plans, it can prove to be a life-saver.

Now let's answer how the strategic planning process should be adopted for its optimal utility. Following are the steps to formulate a business strategy:

1. **Develop a clear vision and translate it into a meaningful mission statement:** Simply put, a vision is a large goal that comes out of the dreams of an entrepreneur, whereas a mission is a milestone or the goal at present towards the achievement of

that vision. The mission may answer the "how" question while vision answers your "why".

2. **Assess the company strength and weaknesses:** Strength is a positive internal factor of a business that can be used to achieve the mission or goal of a company. On the other hand, weaknesses are the internal constraints in achieving those goals.

3. **Scan and analyze the environment for significant business opportunities and threat facing business:** Like point number 2, opportunities are external positive factors while threats are external negative factors.

4. **Identify the key factors for the success of a business:** These are the factors that determine a company's strength and competency to stand in the market and compete. It is also known as a unique selling proposition (USP).

5. **Analyze the competition:** The competition could be of multiple types, but I suggest an analysis of Michele Porter's five forces which are as follows:

   a. Business rivalry

   b. Entry barrier

   c. The threat of substitute

   d. Supplier power

   e. Buyer power

   So, you should conduct a competition analysis basis these factors of the competitive landscape.

6. **Create company goal and objective:** These are objective performance targets and long-range broad milestones.

7. **Formulate the option and choose the most suitable and viable strategy:** This is the roadmap of actions an entrepreneur draws to achieve the objective goal, mission and vision. In general and

also as mentioned in Michele Porter's book 'The Competitive Strategy', there are three major strategies to tackle competition and stand in the market: (a) cost leadership, (b) focus, and (c) differentiation. So, depending upon your strategy, you can either play with the superior quality (differentiation), low cost (cost leadership), or unique customer focus (focus). Decide what suits you the most.

8. **Translate strategy into an action plan**: No strategy is successful unless implemented with the highest precision. So, plan the action, resource, team, training and timing.

9. **Establish accurate tracking and control mechanisms**: Develop proper control and a tracking mechanism. This may include specific MIS in an organization, exception reporting, and taking corrective measures promptly.

I must mention one more thing here that a small business has a big advantage as compared to big business as far as the organization hierarchy goes. Bureaucracy kills the speed of decision-making in these bigger size organizations. Unlike big enterprises, a small business can take advantage of the small resource base, flexible management style, informal organizational structure and adaptability to change. In small business, you may introduce the following relevant customizations:

a.   Use a shorter planning horizon

b.   Do not over-structure but adopt a shirt-sleeve approach

c.   Encourage employee participation

d.   Do not set objectives but evolve through brainstorming with key people and then you will also enjoy immediate buying and fewer restraints

e.   Invest more time in thinking about how to link the day-to-day working with goals and objectives rather than planning

I hope you have understood that strategic management has more to do with the overall direction of the business, target setting, variance analysis and performance management. It encompasses the overall brain power and wisdom of the company and makes it future-ready to fight any uncertainty. It is dynamic and not static as static plans, anyway, do not work in the long run.

Remember, *"the change is the only constant be it life or business planning."*

Chapter 3.2

Ratio Analysis

Ratio analysis is an analytical tool that is used to check various operational aspects of a business. We take up the information from the

financial statement and compare various figures by correlating them to check the solvency, risk, profitability and growth.

A single ratio is never sufficient to know the financial situation of a business. Ratios must be analyzed along with other relevant ratios and then may be compared with their respective previous year ratios. One may also do an industry level comparison or that with a successful competitor. It is imperative to note that ratios work like indicators and parameters, and they are not precise or absolute measurements of any aspect of a business. One should always attempt to know the facts behind a good or bad ratio rather than concluding anything based on a standalone ratio.

The purpose of ratio analysis is to evaluate management performance in terms of profitability, efficiency and risk.

Ratio analysis can be done using the following three methods:

1. **Vertical analysis**: It shows the relationship of each amount to a base figure in a given financial statement. Example, net profit turnover ratio where the turnover is a constant figure (profit and loss account) or current assets when compared to current liabilities (balance sheet), etc.

2. **Horizontal analysis**: Compare two different years for respective percentage change. For example, how the working capital ratios are moving over the last three years. Basically, this amounts to trend analysis.

3. **Ratio analysis:** This puts a different number from a mixed perspective. For example, the fixed assets turnover ratio defines how the plant and machinery are being used year on year to generate sales.

Let's see a broad categorization of ratios (this is not a fixed list and one can also approach various available figures in financial statements and may find a logical relationship between two random figures).

Solvency Ratio	Performance Ratio	Risk Ratio
Liquidity Ratio ▪ Current ratio ▪ Quick ratio ▪ Cash ratio	Operating efficiency ratio ▪ Asset turnover ratio ▪ Equity turnover ratio ▪ Working capital turnover ratio	Financial Risk ▪ Debt to equity ratio ▪ Interest coverage ratio ▪ Debt service coverage ratio

Turnover Ratio	Profitability Ratio	Business Risk
• Debtor turnover • Working capital turnover • Inventory turnover ratio • Creditor turnover ratio • Cash cycle	• Gross profit ratio • Net profit turnover ratio • Return on total assets • Return on total equity • Return on shareholder fund	• Operating leverage • Financial leverage • Total leverage

A sum-up of all the indicators mentioned above are as follows:

1. **Current ratio:** This is a quick, intuitive and easy measure to understand the relationship between the current assets (CA) and current liabilities (CL). The formulae for the current ratio is CA divided by CL. The higher the ratio, the better is the liquidity. The current ratio of 1 is considered good and if it is more than 1.5, then it indicates the non-optimization of resources. If the current assets consist of major receivable or chunks of an old investor, you should be cautious of its liquidity. These days, people have also been appreciative of negative working capital wherein this ratio is seen more as an efficiency management parameter than liquidity measurement.

2. **Quick ratio:** This is a stricter version of the current ratio wherein the inventory is taken out from current Assets on the pretext that inventory converting into cash takes a little longer, so the same may not be readily available for offsetting any immediate current liability. The quick ratio is calculated by dividing current assets (further reduced by inventory) with current liabilities.

This is also known as the acid test ratio. The low quick ratio (as compared to standard) indicates liquidity problems in the short term.

3. **Cash ratio:** This is the strictest liquidity measurement. Here, in current assets, we count only the cash, bank and immediate liquid securities like stocks saleable in the stock market. This ratio is used, to analyze the liquidity issue if any in a very short time (less than a month).

4. **Debtor turnover:** This ratio indicates the relation between the sale and receivable and the outcome is the number of cycles of credit sale converting into cash in a defined time cycle. It can be calculated either quarterly or annually. Here we take credit sale as the numerator and average receivables as the denominator. This is also used for calculating the debtor turnover in a day, which is also called the average collection period. It is calculated by dividing 365 with debtor turnover.

5. **Inventory turnover ratio:** An inventory turnover ratio can be used to measure the efficiency of a business as far as the conversion of inventory (including raw material and WIP) into sales is concerned. In general, higher inventory turnover indicates better performance, whereas a lower turnover indicates inefficiency. Here, instead of counting the sale value of finished goods, we count the cost of goods sold. There is also a trend of counting this ratio in terms of days (calculated by dividing 365 by inventory turnover ratio).

6. **Creditor turnover ratio:** Creditors or payables turnover indicates the number of times that payables are rotated during the specified period. It is best measured against purchases (only credit purchase ideally) since purchases generate accounts payable. Again, we use the cost of goods sold and inventories, etc. at cost price and not the sale price. So the formula to know

payable turnover is purchases divided by average accounts payable. For the calculation of days, we divide 365 by payable turnover ratio. Higher payable turnover days indicate lower working capital deployment and thus, better efficiency.

7. **Cash cycle:** The overall business runs on a model as to how fast the outflow can be converted into bigger inflow (that is cost plus profit). The overall time is taken from outflow to inflow in called cash cycle and is the pure-play of debtors turnover days (A), inventory turnover days (B) and payable turnover days (C). The total cash cycle is A+B-C.

8. **Asset turnover ratio:** This ratio measures the optimization level of assets of a business. This is calculated by dividing the total sale by total assets that have been put to use. The ratio varies substantially depending upon the nature of the industry, therefore be cautious while you compare two different companies or industries. For example, the manufacturing industry shall have a lower ratio as compared to the service sector.

9. **Equity turnover ratio:** This is to measure the efficiency of equity capital as far as sales are concerned. The equity turnover ratio is calculated by dividing the total sales with an average of total equity capital. The ratio varies substantially depending upon how capital-intensive the business/industry is. Thus, a power generating business may have a much lower ratio than a services sector business, since the power plant requires a much larger capital investment. Be cautious while you compare two companies look at capital investment some that belong to different industries.

10. **Working capital turnover:** The working capital turnover ratio measures how well a company is utilizing its working capital. Working capital is current assets minus current liabilities. A high working capital turnover ratio indicates that the management has

been efficiently using the firm's short-term assets and liabilities to support a high volume of sales. On the contrary, a low ratio indicates non-performance on many fronts.

11. **Gross profit ratio:** Gross profit is the difference between total sales and total direct cost of making a product or providing a service. Please note that costs like administrative overheads, taxes, interests are not deducted here. It is one of the most important ratios and is calculated by dividing the gross profit by sales. The manufacturing overhead like factory rental and manufacturing plant's depreciation could be absorbed in the cost of goods sold but no head of expenses done towards selling the finished goods.

12. **Net profit turnover ratio:** The word 'net profit' is subject to multiple interpretations, and it can shape up among any bottom-line figure starting from EBIT (earnings before interest and taxes). It is calculated by dividing the EBIT or EBT or EAT (earning after tax) by total sales. In general, the net profit means profit after tax but taking EBT as net profit is also quite prevalent. Make sure to use the same benchmark when you compare two ratios from two different companies.

13. **Return on total assets:** The total assets of an organization include both debt and equity. It is also called the total capital invested. Return on total assets is calculated by dividing the EBIT by total assets.

14. **Return on total equity:** Total equity means the totals of common shareholder fund, preference capital, reserves and so all capital except outside debts. As we calculate the profits available for equity shareholders, we take earnings after taxes and divide the same by total equity capital to get the return on total equity.

15. **Return on shareholder fund:** Shareholder fund is defined to be the innermost layer of capital and it excludes the minority as well as preference capital. Accordingly, net profit is not only

after-tax but we also take out the dividend share of minority and preference dividend and then divide the same by only shareholder fund to get the ratio.

16. **Debt to equity ratio:** How much outside debt the company has taken in relation to its use of equity is an important indicator of the company's ability to pay off debts using its own capital. Generally, lower the ratio, the better it is. Debt includes current debt + long term debt. The banker shall not give you loans if you have a high debt-equity ratio. If over a period, the debt to equity ratio has moved upward, then it indicates that the company is not able to generate enough cash in the business and, as a result, is browning more, which is a negative indicator. This ratio is also known as the financial leverage ratio.

17. **Interest coverage ratio:** This ratio indicates the interest-paying capacity of the firm, and so we calculate the coverage by dividing the EBIDTA (earnings before interest, depreciation, taxes and amortization) by total interest payable. This checks how sufficient the operating income of the company is to pay off the interest. The higher it is, the better.

18. **Debt service coverage ratio (DSCR):** Now if in place of just paying the interest, which can be the case of overdraft or cc (cash credit) limit, there could be some repayment of loan too. If we add up this repayment amount to interest, it becomes the total debt service amount and when EBIT is divided with total debt service amount, we get the DSCR. This is a very important calculation for bankers to sanction any loan.

19. **Operating leverage, financial leverage and total leverage:** Leverages measure the percentage movement among the EBIT, EAT and sales. Operating leverage is the comparison of the percentage change in EBIT and sale, financial leverage is a comparison of percentage change net income and EBIT and

total leverage is calculated by multiplying the operating leverage with financial leverage. Hence, the total leverage of business is the percentage change in net income divided by percentage change in the total sale. Operating leverage is a measure of how sensitive the operating income is to the change in revenues. Financial leverage primarily originates from the company's financing decisions (use of debt). Total leverage measures the sensitivity of the net income to sales.

Let's end this chapter with a very important tool that is used to analyze the overall business health and is known as the DuPont analysis (named after DuPont Corporation). DuPont analysis is also used to decompose the different drivers of return on equity (ROE). An investor can use analysis like this to compare the operational efficiency of two similar firms.

DuPont Analysis=Net Profit Margin × Asset Turnover × Assets leverage

wherein,

Net profit margin tells you the operating efficiency,

Asset turnover indicates the optimal use of assets and

Assets leverage indicates how capable the company is to finance the purchase of new assets

If you put the formulas here, the net result you get is the return on equity therefore this analysis is also called the DuPont ROE model.

Capital Structure and Shareholder Value

There are two primary sources of funds at the macro level in any company i.e. debt (having a fixed obligation of paying interest) and equity (part of shareholder and owner capital). We all know that the end objective of running any business is to maximize the value of shareholders or equity owners. So, whether to use the owner's equity capital or use the company credential to raise debt is always a tricky decision and the same calls for some in-depth knowledge of the correlation between these two major categories of finance.

As debt is an outside liability, the resultant interest is a third-party cost and is allowed as the cost of doing business, and so has the taxation benefit while calculating the taxable income of the company. On the other hand, the dividend paid to owners is always paid after the payment of third-party liabilities and taxes.

So whether to go for debt or equity mode calls for a comparison of the cost involved in these funds and their final effect on the PAT (profit after tax which is available for the dividend to owners). There are multiple theories available for analyzing this correlation. However, when we analyze the operating statement of companies at large, we need to run logical mathematics and see the various level of operating profits and related tax benefits. Basically, we have to reach a break-even point where the earning to shareholders becomes indifferent irrespective of the mode of finance. This is also called EPS or PBIT analysis for capital structure decisions. In an improved analysis, we may also reach an indifference point in the correlation between return on investment (ROI) and return on equity (ROE). So the finish line is a point at which capital structures make the maximum distributable amount available for the owners and that's all.

We also may use the leverage (operating, financial and total leverage) and ratio analysis (debt service coverage and interest service coverage) to complete and support the capital structure decisions, but it is better for now that we keep ourselves to only basic tools of capital structure.

The capital structure, as mentioned earlier, is a tough decision and is an act of balancing among its various constituents like income, cost, risk, control, flexibility, credentials, and time. To decide on an ideal capital structure, the following guidelines may be useful:

a. Take full advantage of tax benefits, which will finally reduce the cost of finance

b. Take appropriate funds at the appropriate stages of your business. For example, you cannot opt for IPO while you are in the first year of business or you cannot ask for seed funds when you have a mature business.

c. Keep your business flexible and do not opt for debt raise in the first instance. Debt can be raised quickly as compared to equity, so you may like to preserve those capacities for the urgent need of funds. Do not block your leverage.

d. Raise money when you have the ideal circumstances and not when you are dying out. So, take financial decisions proactively and well in advance.

e. Look for optimal capital structure for your business and by optimal I mean the structure at which the earning per share is maximum and weightage average cost of capital is minimum

f. There could be legal constraints and regulations for raising debt and equity in the country of operation. Make sure to comply with those guidelines.

g. The purpose of raising funds and the cost of funds must be compared to look at the possible ROI and then the time of deployment of these funds, and the cost of raising such funds (processing cost) should be considered in detail.

h. There should be a minute analysis of control being diluted as per the terms and conditions set by investors, and it should be calibrated keeping in mind the personal consideration and cash flow ability of the company.

i. You must consider the market condition while deciding the structure. The market condition should be favourable for the selected fund. As the market condition keeps fluctuating—bullish or bearish—it has a direct impact on your capital raising decisions.

j. You must also consider issuing innovative securities that are quasi in nature rather than plain. So combining the need and availability and creating a blend is a good idea. For example, rather than issuing equity or debenture, you may consider issuing convertible debentures if that is a fulfilling solution.

k. Consider the international market as and when appropriate and practical. Good treasury function can help here to identify a better market to raise funds.

Some of the well-researched and widely used theories of capital structure are Modigliani and Miller model, Pecking Order theory, WACC and HAMADA model.

The capital structure decisions are often linked to the sensitivity of funds to economic cycles, asset intensity and other similar factors. Analyzing capital structure in isolation provides limited insights, and hence it is suggested to analyze the global, country and geography position along with peer groups of companies to reach at target ideal capital structure.

The objective of capital structure analysis is to identify the range of structures based on which the company's overall cost of capital is minimized and is in the best interest of the company looking at all factors discussed earlier. When the current capital structure is away from the target structure, the company should evaluate all prospective sources of funds and assess how future financing decisions will move the company's present capital structure to its target. Migrating from the existing capital structure to a target capital structure is often a gradual process and should not be rushed.

To conclude the relationship between the cost of capital and shareholder value (enterprise value or firm value, which we will discuss in the next chapter), let me give you a summary note of enterprise value. The enterprise value in the case of start-up/operating companies is calculated primarily basis the market capitalization or the income approach wherein the future cash flows of business are discounted at cost of capital. If the cost of capital is low, the value shall be higher as both are inversely proportional.

So, the cost of capital does not only help to enhance the net profit of the company year on year but also has a direct role in determining the discount factor for enterprise valuation. The lower the cost of capital, the higher is the enterprise valuation and so the shareholder value. But remember one thing that the cost of capital should not be reduced by leveraging the company beyond a point as the same shall increase the risk premium, which devalues the company in the immediate future. Highly leveraged companies are always more prone to insolvency and face the risk of instability.

So, the best cost of capital must meet the criterion of being the cheapest as well as least leveraged and only then you can count it as real equilibrium for enhancing the shareholder's value.

Chapter 3.4

Corporate Valuation Management

As value maximization is the central idea behind running a successful enterprise and having worthy management, so it is important for managers and leaders to understand the tool and techniques that can help in measuring and managing the corporate value.

In the earlier section, we read about basic ideas and methodologies of valuation, and now we are going to discuss few value-based management tools. We will focus on up and running business more than those which need special attention, like firms that have cyclical nature or are in distress and liquidation.

Among all the available approaches of valuation (market-based, income-based and cost-based), the income approach is most followed and widely used. While market multiple approaches are equally good for comparison and further assurance of the fair valuation, the one, which counts the future cash flows during the entire life cycle, is most important and the same is called Discounted Cash Flow (DCF). Since the early 90s, the DCF model has received greater acceptance with leading investment banking firms and HNIs due to the sheer superiority of the concept and its simplicity.

The DCF is an improved model over the other traditional models like earning capitalization, etc. Various models got developed over a period of time by different economists, but the basic vision remains the same as to how to reach the nearest value of all probable cash in-flows and then the calculation of the present value as on the date of calculation. The discounted cash flow approach to value a company passes through the following steps:

1. Analyzing the subject company's history with regard to performance and stability

2. Calculating and finalizing the nearest applicable cost of capital

3. Basis all possible knowledge about the economy, industry and past performance of the company, forecasting the performance for three to 15 years. The period that can be forecasted with reasonable certainty is called an explicit period.

4. Determining the continuing value of performance and growth model perspective. There could be a single (constant one growth rate during the entire life cycle), double (an initial period of high growth and then getting stability) or three (an initial high, a transition low and then stable) growth in different time zones of life of the company.

5. Calculating the value of a firm by discounting all future earnings assuming it to be a never lasting business. We call that perpetuity value.

6. Interpreting the resultant value and analyzing the same in the right perspective

The very next practical aspect for valuation is estimating/counting the viable cash flows, and as the model indicates, it is not billing or profit but free cash flow.

The cash flow could be calculated differently depending upon the fact whether the valuation is being done for the overall firm or only for equity owners. In valuing the enterprise for equity, shareholder and owner fund, we always count the free cash flow to equity (FCFE). On the other hand, in the valuation of enterprise overall, which we call firm value or enterprise value, we take free cash flow to the firm (FCFF). I choose to leave the further description of FCFF and FCFE at this level and not getting into further technicality to keep the subject simple and interesting.

There are few broad and macro guidelines while you are calculating and interpreting the corporate valuation:

a. Understand all possible approaches and models and choose at least two different approaches

b. Always believe in the valuation number to be in a range rather than a static sacrosanct number

c. Check the forecast one more time as the forecasted numbers are also your minimum performance commitment

d. Avoid back-calculation to make the forecast suitable for expected wishful valuation

e. Use the different strategies of valuation for different objectives and circumstances. For example, the corporate valuation for issuing new securities could be different than a possible merger transaction.

f. It is always the fair value (not high or low) that counts most, which is defined as the practical transaction value in an efficient market without any undue pressure on the buyer or seller.

To help companies enhance their valuation and in turn the value for their shareholder, there a few concepts that are known as value-based management (VBM).

Many leading corporate giants have adopted many of these models with value creation as their central idea. The value comes out of special opportunity and competitive advantage a corporate may have in the market. The strategies to know, analyze and use those specific advantages for their best future, become a management practice (VBM) and these practices have even been named in the name of those companies. For example, the ALCAR approach is named after the name of the company itself M/s Alcar Group Inc.

Value-based management runs on basic premises that the conventional return on investments as per accounting books does not take into account the business risk, opportunity cost of capital and finally the present value of future returns over a specified period.

There are following three principal methods of VBM:

A. Free cash flow method proposed by McKinsey/Alcar group (FCF/DCF)

B. Economic value added or market value added as proposed by Stern Stewart and Co. (EVA or MVA)

C. Cash value added (CVA) as proposed by the Boston Consulting group

ALCAR approach/shareholder value add (SVA model) suggest the following seven value drivers that affect the shareholder value:

Operating factors

a. Rate of growth of revenue/sale

b. Operating income margins

c. Duration of income

d. Income tax rates

Investment factors

e. Capital investment

f. Working capital

Financing factor

g. The cost of capital is dependent upon the associated risk of the project

A successful SVA means the implementation of strategies that maximize the value for shareholders and plan all expenses on such achievement, and when there are no such opportunities, return the cash to shareholders. Once invested in a business, the owner does not really appreciate the capital being refunded and neither this is practical, and hence the SVA model looks very old school.

Stern Stewart (EVA model): This is the most widely used model in today's corporate world. It simply takes into account the surplus left for owners or equity holders after discharging all possible third-party interests and expenses including the government taxes. The surplus so left is the economic value added (EVA) for owners.

This can be shown as follows:

$$EVA = NOPAT - (WACC \times Capital)$$

Whereas,

EVA - Economic Value Added

NOPAT - Net operating profit after tax

Unlike accounting practices, we capitalize on many of the preliminary and deferred revenue expenses rather than treating them as the cost for the annual period.

WACC - Weightage average cost of capital

Like the Alcar model, this also takes into account the value drivers that are components of reaching the free surplus. Higher the profit after tax, the higher is the EVA. For example, the cost of capital here is the weightage average cost of capital, which demands a good financial structure to drive the EVA. Even expenses like compensation and incentive are linked to EVA rather than the business target or margins target, etc. The concept of Market Value Added (MVA) is nothing but the present value of all future EVAs, therefore it is taken just as a necessary extension of the EVA model.

Boston Consulting Group (BCG): This approach is a blend of two concepts i.e. cash flow returns on investment and cash value added (CVA)

The performance is measured on the following two fronts:

1. **Total shareholder return (TSR):** This takes into account the capital appreciation of shareholder's stocks and dividends earned by them. This is very well accepted in investment communities.

2. **Total business return (TBR):** This is the internal calculation of returns in business and on which the TSR is based. It is needed for managing the management compensations and check on their performance and other strategic decisions. The TBR is calculated on the basic concept of diminishing returns in business (over a period of time) and is also known as a time fade model.

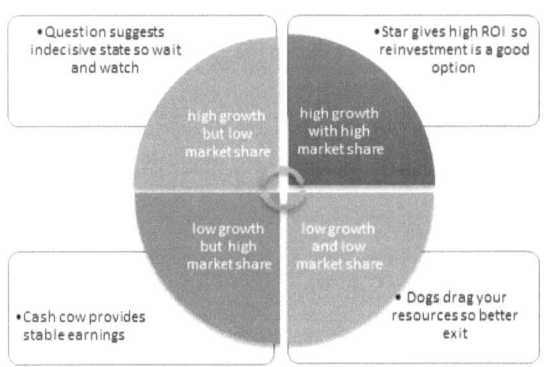

The BCG model uses the cash flow return on investment matrix and basis that the strategic decision of investments or exits is made. The BCG matrix is essentially divided into four quadrants between market growth and relative market share.

Cash cows: These are the businesses in low growth markets with high market share. This segment is the best to be in, and it simply means to milk the cow as long as possible without killing it.

Dogs: These are products with low growth and low market share. It is advised to withdraw from this product/business and focus your resources elsewhere.

Stars: These are the products/businesses in high growth markets with a high market share. This quadrant is considered a good ROI model. It may require investment and that must be done to sustain the position and enhance cash value add.

Question marks or problem child: These are the products in high growth markets with low market share. This quadrant suggests an indecisive status of a business and probably asks you to wait and watch for some time.

Most of the big companies have been adopting the VBM around the globe but from all those early adoptions and present modules of customization, we can learn the following basics tips pertaining to the successful implementation of VBM.

- This must have support from the top management and the employees should be educated about it.

- The incentive and compensations should be made an integral part of VBM.

- The metrics chosen should be practical and viable. One size does not fit all. Customize the plan.

- On a concluding note, the VBM must start in an organization with value-based leadership, which simply means leading the team and evaluating performance—both for the leaders and the teams—based on the organization's set parameters (SVA, EVA, CVA) rather than specific metrics and milestones set by individual leaders. Also, ensure that the corporate culture is in sync with value creation disciplines. Everyone, starting from leader to team member, must adhere to those disciplines and manifest the same in everything they say and do.

Chapter 3.5

How to Handle Competition

Competition is usually seen with a negative outlook, but competition is good not only for the customers but for the business as well. Competition works against the monopolization of any product in the industry and it is the competition risk that products and services are enhanced and improved to protect the respective market shares. If customers like some service or product, then they will start using it more frequently and this is how the business ramps up. Looking at this growth and ROI, other competitors would enter into the market and more competitors in the same field would bring economies of scale, which means better quality at economical prices. In the end, it is a win-win situation for both businesses and customers at large.

Business competition is something that always exists irrespective of the place or product. Sometimes it may be lesser/healthy or more/fierce. The purpose of the competition is to make the market share and then protect/maintain/increase it. It is all about the volume of sales, and margins follow due to operating efficiencies and economies of scale. There could be multiple types of competition like direct or indirect, replacement or substitution, etc. The business competition amounts to more pressure on resources including the talent pool and at times creates an unnecessary drain on the profitability of the company and too many identical direct competitors even create confusion for the customer. But it also facilitates the privilege of choosing better quality at cheaper prices and so induces innovation, research and creativity.

Depending upon the geography and economy, there could be multiple types of competition starting from perfect competition to oligopoly and monopoly. In general, a monopoly is considered anti-customer/anti-public and so unless, there is a very valid reason like patent right or public service, monopoly is not allowed in any economy. In India, we used to have laws to restrict such monopolistic practices in the form of the Monopolies and Restrictive Trade Practices Act 1969, which was replaced by the Competition Act 2003. The Act was amended in 2007, and it now enlists all the unfair trade practices as well as Anti-Competitive Agreements and abuse of dominance. In other words, a marketplace having perfect competition is appreciated both by customers as well as businesses and government.

To identify and analyze the competitive forces that affect every industry, do a strength and weakness study (SWOT) and other related go-to-market strategies. There is an old and trusted fundamental theory called the Five Forces Model, also known as **Porter's model** and

the five forces model, named after Harvard Business School professor, Michael E. Porter. The pretext of the model is that the business competition risk is not always the direct existing competition having similar offerings but the future risk of fierce competition that should be kept in mind to come up with a long-term business strategy.

As per Porter's model, there are following five forces that play a pivot role in defining the competitive landscape and building a long-term plan.

1. **Industries present competitors**: These are existing competitors and provide the same product or service. The fact that these competitors exist generally tends to have a deflating effect on profits. The higher the intensity of rivalry, the more important it is for the business to have a sustainable competitive advantage to protect its market share and profits.

2. **Potential new entrants and entry barriers**: These are future competitors that are yet come into the market. They are attracted to a profit-making market and unless there are strong entry barriers, the extra/super profit being earned by the companies is taken away by these new entrants.

3. **Risk of substitution:** These are products or services that are not the same as those produced by the current business but are so similar in nature that they may replace the usage of existing products and bring down the market share and profits of the company.

4. **Power of suppliers**: When there is a monopoly or strong suppliers/groups that are more powerful than the business, they tend to dictate terms of business, delivery, quantities, price, quality, etc. If the company/industry is making significant profits, the supplier may ask to increase the supply price, which would have a diminishing effect on the profits.

5. **Power of buyers:** When buyers (customers) are more powerful than the business, they tend to dictate terms of business. If the business is making significant profits, the buyer could insist on more economical prices, which would again reduce the profit.

Even though Porter's model is not a risk assessment model for corporate industries, it is one of the most important tools for doing SWOT on the macro/industry level. In the Harvard Business Review Article, Porter wrote, "Understanding the competitive forces and their underlying causes reveals the roots of an industry's current profitability while providing a framework for anticipating and influencing competition (and profitability) over time."

There is an old saying that "never underestimate your competitor" and also that "better to look and improve inside than looking at the whole world and getting frustrated". As we understand about the competition and its nature, necessity, limitation, type, advantage and disadvantage, let's understand as to how to handle competition to our advantage so that it becomes a fighting force rather than a cause of concern:

a. Know your target customer in full and build a special relationship through one or another tool. The tool to be used may differ from business to business and I leave that to you.

b. Understand and focus on the subject and nuances of competition and not on the competitor. Many a time we keep obsessing over the size and might of the competitor and ignore the subject of differentiation.

c. You need to be focused on the quality of your deliverables and clear communication tools should be adopted to differentiate your offerings as compared to your competitors.

d. Keep research, knowledge sharing and other reaches out program always live and floating to maintain active engagement with your customers.

e. You may also explore new market segments if the offerings allow so, but this exploration should not cost your old customer base.

f. You should also look out for some association opportunities and sharing of research, etc. with your competitors. There could be situations wherein competitors could use each other's services in a few aspects. For example, in high season, the unused production capacity of one competitor could be used for another, which is a win-win situation for both.

g. Keep innovating and keep your worth intact by looking at both internal (employees) and external (customers) clients and keeping them happy and satisfied.

Chapter 3.6

Cash and Liquidity Management

Cash is the most liquid asset in any business across the segment and stage. Appropriate cash balance makes you fly or even crash if mishandled. We all know that cash is needed for monetary transactions and taking care of any immediate or contingent need, but it has its own opportunity cost too. So the business should make a plan and estimate the receipts and payments for the future period for maintaining optimal utilization of such liquid resources. A high cash level does not necessarily mean an optimum level.

So what is the optimal cash level of any business?

We understand that cash is needed for doing many things in business, and we also know that the cash lying unutilized shall have the opportunity cost. So, we generally invest the surplus into marketable securities or liquid bonds and other similar securities. When we need cash, we end up selling those securities to generate cash. The process of conversion of securities into cash has a transaction cost, and it is inversely proportional to the size of cash reserve. We need to observe the movement of these two costs in line with the quantum of cash reserve. So the optimal cash level is the break-even point between the transaction cost and opportunity cost. There are various cash models like Baumol Model and Miller & Orr Model to gauze such optimal break-even points.

The basic principles of optimal cash management are as follows:

a.   Adopt a good **cash forecasting** and estimation system

b.   Initiate simple and periodical **cash report**s

c.   Do not allow **idle cash** at any point in time

d.   **Collect as fast as possible** even at the cost of cash discounts

e.   Maintain a healthy **relationship with bankers**

f.   Modernize the **receipt and payment mechanics**

g.   Develop and use the **short term borrowings**

Let's look at the principles in detail for better understanding.

Cash forecasting

This is one of the major tools of cash management, and it includes making of policies towards the preservation and estimation of inflow and outflow. This may include the cash requirements for a specified period, short-term financing, scheduling of outward payments, purchases of raw material, cash credits and employees petty cash payments. One of the most used methods of forecasting is making of receipt and payment statement for the forecasted period to the best of estimates and then following it to a T (doing it absolutely perfect). This statement has nothing to do with the accounting entries and treatment of inflow for final accounts. This is also called a cash flow statement.

While estimating the fund flow and bringing discipline in the company, this method of forecasting does not take into account the uncertainty caused by third parties like vendors or clients. In short, no probability wisdom is used here, therefore at times, it cannot be considered to be the most reliable forecast even though it is widely used.

Cash reporting

Cash reports provide a variance statement of the actual cash flow as compared to the forecasted one and are helpful in controlling and revising/rescheduling the fund flows to adapt to the scenario change. In general, we adopt the following three such reports in our management information system (MIS):

a. **Daily cash statement:** Opening balance, receipts, payments and closing balance of cash and bank

b. **Weekly cash reports:** Along with items mentioned in daily cash reports, this statement also counts the change in other immediately realizable assets like receivables and scheduled payment liabilities.

c. **Monthly cash summary:** Here we amplify the weekly reports into monthly and present a variance analysis as compared to forecast and also carryover of receipts rights and payment obligations. One may explore the corrective actions here that may be necessary for next month's forecast to match the cash budget matrix.

No idle cash

Idle cash or idle money as the name implies is the cash that is sitting idle and has not been put to use or earning any income. Cash is usually the currency that acts as a legal tender in business. However, for idle cash calculation, we include cash equivalents lying in the current accounts or elsewhere where no interest/income is being generated.

One can use idle money by either investing in an interest-bearing instrument, buying a productive asset, or even short-term lending. An investor must select the option on the basis of their need, risk appetite, and financial goals. The following are the options where one can park their idle money:

1. Money multiplier accounts where the balances are made term deposits and are utilized as and when the fund is needed leaving the unused part to continue to earn interest. This is something that should be done by all businesses and, in particular, all the funded Start-ups to have some financial income too.

2. Overdraft against fixed deposits also provides a tool for saving and many bankers offer this.

3. Stock market liquid funds and arbitrage funds

4. Discount earnings wherein you may offer to the vendor to pay before the due date against some cash discounts. This helps maintain a better operating profit.

Collect as fast as possible

Collecting fast in any business plays a crucial role in the sustenance of business in the short as well as long run. A collection strategy is an important tool towards cash and liquidity management, and it talks about the discipline an organization maintains. Few important factors which have a long-drawn impact on the success of such strategies are as follows:

1. Restrictive credit benchmarks

2. Tracking system for due dates and strict protocol for overdue payments

3. Avoid extended credit terms and build a cash discount in pricing strategy

4. Have a model of advance payments or midway biilings, than arrears

5. Base all business incentives on collection rather than billings

6. Keep the line of steps to be taken on overdue payments simple and fluid for the collection manager

7. Do not hesitate much on legal recourse as the client who does not pay rightly is not a good client. Of course, before the initiation of the legal process, all other options should be exhausted.

Relationship with bankers

The nature of your relationship with your bankers goes a long way irrespective of the borrowing needs. I suggest having some kind of borrowing relationship, however symbolic it may be, as it helps you during the hours of need and also builds your  credentials for enhanced future borrowings for better financial leverage. If you have a friendly relationship, you get benefited not only in terms of the preferred rate of interest but also the ease of doing business, faster credits of instruments, better exchange rates and knowledge of novel product of credit lines which can benefit you. As the banker lends you, they take a certain risk and they get interested in your success too, thus a good banker works like an advocate for your business. Their business shall be good only when your business does well. They are also active in the business community, and, at times, they may help you to connect with your prospect. A banking relationship is a crucial business relationship for all sizes of business and specifically for SME.

Modernize the receipts and payments process

Even though the cheque clearing system continues to exist, there has been an upsurge in the digital payment system and the same should be adopted wherever possible. This helps you to reduce the float size in your business and be more liquid at any given point of time. The usability of your money gets enhanced and collection time reduces. If opted well, the collection cycle can simply be reduced by three days and creditors' payments too can be optimized for saving three days. In total, a week's time saving of even just the gross margin can help your business immensely, and if you have a good investment model, then you may end up earning a good amount of interest during this float time. Also, if you have a good business banking relationship and appropriate transaction size, these functions can be outsourced to bankers to save the manpower costs.

Short-term borrowings

The means and mechanism of short-term borrowings should be developed and made flexible and readily available. Again, I suggest having a credit line with any bank or financial institution on an ongoing basis irrespective of the present need. The products like invoice factoring, bill discounting and overdraft facility to finance your receivables must be there, on as and when needed basis.

In recent years, the importance and use of cash and liquidity management had increased dramatically therefore, to maintain a robust system of cash management, the primary elements like collection, disbursements, optimum cash balance, short-term investment guidelines and proper tracking system must be taken care of. Liquidity is the number one factor of business management these days and having a long list of debtors is not considered good at all. Your rightful money should be timely available for your business, and it should not be dependent upon someone else's decision, situation and capacity.

Chapter 3.7

Performance Management System

Performance management system (PMS) is an organized and systematic way of setting goals and objectives for employees, conducting a periodic review, recognizing and rewarding the achievements of employees, providing feedback for better performance and implementing employee development programs.

The basic purpose of PMS is to improve the corporate performance by improving the employee's productivity, and it can result in an overall benefit not only for the organization but also for the line manager and employees. While the overall productivity of the business increases as it generates better returns on the money spent on manpower, it also adds to cost-cutting, retention and loyalty of employees, which has its own long-term benefits. For the line manager or supervisors, it saves their time and energy and increases their bandwidth to do more work for better output. For employees, job satisfaction goes high, and the appreciation comes

in the form of not only better compensation but also high morale and self-confidence.

PMS is a continuous process that is carried out right from the time when an employee is on-boarded in an organization until the time he/she leaves it. The followings are the pillars of PMS:

1. The selection process, outlines and defines the objective of getting the best, suitable candidate under the company's budget. It also includes clearly defined job description key responsibility area (KRA) before you start interviewing the shortlisted candidates.

2. Careful deliberation and communicating the KRA and key performance indicators (KPI) to the selected candidate helps in setting the right goals. In order to have a positive work environment, the goals should be clear, measurable and achievable.

3. Conducting training sessions for the selected candidates for optimum productivity

4. Conducting periodic review and feedback mechanism which is possible only when you have a measurable goal index.

5. Setting up a performance incentive system and super-achiever bonus for performances beyond fixed benchmarks. Any specific goal when achieved must be recognized and rewarded.

6. Defining a good exit process that includes a detailed exit interview so that any deficiency at the organization front could be improved and resolved. The outgoing employee can share some valuable advice to improve the performance as there is no fear of any consequential damage.

Research has shown that performance review systems tend to focus on the past, and the same results in demotivation for those employees who could not perform well in the past due to any pressing issues.

This does not mean that the system should be thrown out or it is useless, but if the PMS is prepared considering its drawbacks, it can help the organization and employees in the right direction. The followings can be said to be the backbone for the success of a dynamic PMS:

a. The system should elevate employee performance and not just measure their performance against the lower benchmarks. The system should rather talk about wilful responsibility than making someone accountable. Responsibility amounts to empowerment whereas accountability sounds more like punishment.

b. The system should be made in such a way that the overall compensation becomes a by-product of PMS. In a traditional setup, hierarchy/position often beats the performance, however, the reverse is true and people have started realizing it.

c. PMS should use multiple data points for its efficacy and timely decision than an annual affair wherein facts like accountability, compensation, and retention are based on the past rather than the latest factor. The line manager being biased is a common reason for high employee turnover. Along with the line manager's reports, the monthly reports, HR initiative and training inputs, co-worker attitude, one-to-one meeting, quarterly check-in, and loyalty must be considered too.

d. The system should not only be fair and efficient but also flexible, lucid and simple. The review should be subjective while one talks about the working environment but should be objective while evaluating the performance. Ticking the box with an intelligent matrix is always better than subjective discussions and the biased perception of the supervising manager. The system should count both the mechanics in an intelligent way and certain weightage should be given to all possible inputs. As a leader, adapting to the level and quality of feedback and being able to synthesize data from multiple sources is critical.

e. The system must integrate regular feedback communication to employees and also the training and coaching programs based on the feedback. This shall certainly help the employee towards career enhancement and the manager to create a larger talent pool of engaged, motivated and loyal employees. Creating peer benchmarking and providing a level of transparency for employees to see their progress against their own peer group can prove vital here due to the basic longing to compete and win in all of us.

Most of the performance reviews leave the employees demotivated and tired than inspired, leading to increased staff turnover. Therefore, progressive companies are now leaving these annual performance appraisals and adopting a feedback culture with regular check-ins. Some of the leading companies that have adopted this culture of constant feedback include Deloitte, Microsoft, GE, Dell and Adobe. It comes as no surprise that these companies regularly attract the most talented manpower. Their employees receive regular feedback, which helps them improve themselves and become more efficient and capable.

Coming at tools of performance management, the technologies have taken the burden and software is being developed to encompass all the pre-requisites of balanced and continuous feedback and appraisal process. Nowadays, it is possible to streamline goal-setting via digital processes in a way that has objectives synced with data-analytics on actual business performance and which can be altered as needed in real-time. All these tools aim to improve performance by empowering and substantiating the employee-manager discourse and focusing on the same. At many places, the gamification of the overall process has started wherein the challenges are accepted and goals are set for certain exciting rewards.

In short, the PMS should be customized, result-oriented, adaptable, time-bound and real-time, with precise action points for achievable and measurable goals, and finally part of the reward and recognition program of the organization.

Chapter 3.8

Business Hygiene Audit

While multiple types of mandatory and recommendatory audits happen in your business, it is suggested that you, as a business owner, have your own method of checking business hygiene.

Annual Statutory audit in case of LLC (LLP above certain turnover) and tax audits (under the Income Tax Act if your total billing exceeds a prefixed slab) are few compulsory audits. Internal audit/management audit/project audit/thrust area based audits are few examples of third-party audit you generally get conducted in your business to understand the compliances and standard of working. A third-party audit is a costly affair and too frequent audits also pose a work slowdown risk. What is suggested here is to maintain your own internal check and control points for various departments, and you may just need a few administrative and

coordinating skill sets to get the data for your perusal, or depending upon the organization structure, your assistant can do it.

Even during audits by third-party professionals, these are the important points of reference and those professional auditors shall then explain to you the reasons, environment and interpretations of these data points. It is important to keep in mind that nobody understands your business more than you, and a third party should be engaged only if there is a paucity of bandwidth at your end or there is a complete lack of financial skill set or there is an issue of priority setting.

I am going to discuss and give you a few extremely important pointers reading through which you may judge the efficacy and compliance management of your business on a macro level. If you notice any problem, then you may hire a professional auditor/consultant to do a microanalysis and find a solution. These important points (department-wise) of reference and suggestions for better internal control and a controlled working environment are as follows:

General company outlook

1. You must have an organization chart depicting the departments and key officers with a hierarchy who are accountable for smooth functioning.

2. You should have standard operating procedures that should be made as per the practical work needs rather than ideology. Among others, the accounting manual and employee handbooks are must documents.

3. There should be a healthy and periodical management information system for review purposes. In MIS, few reports could be daily and few could be weekly or monthly.

4. There should be a budgetary control mechanism for expenses as well as revenue.

5. The software being used should be licensed.

6. If there is manual document generation, then there should be a plan for the digitalization of these manual records and back up thereof.

7. Registration certificates and relevant licenses should be displayed at appropriate places, and there should also be a notice board for multiple purposes even though it may sound old-fashioned.

8. An appropriate and adequate insurance must be taken for plant, stock, cash and people.

9. Secretarial and legal, including taxation schedules, must be followed at all cost as statutory non-compliance leads to many complications, including the blacklisting for possible loans in the market and banks.

Cash

1. Check if you have petty cash and the main cash system in place. Petty cash maintenance helps you to have a better grip on the most liquid assets of the company, and then your main accountant can control it on a day-to-day basis by closing the petty cash every day.

2. The physical verification of cash with two signatories who are accountable for cash/petty cash maintenance and cash receipt and payment is crucial every day irrespective of nil transactions.

3. The company cash should never be mixed with the personal cash of your accountant to avoid the failure of internal check-point and facilitate the early detection of unauthorized use of company resources.

4. The authority matrix for approval of cash payment and the quantum of physical cash being maintained should be crystal clear. The amount above the pre-fixed upper limit should immediately be deposited in the bank.

5. You must have cash in the safe as well as cash in transit insurance in place with the name of the cash handler mentioned in the policy to avoid any complication.

6. An acknowledgment of receipt must be given for all over the counter (OTC) receipts, and these OTC receipts should be serially numbered and should be kept safe.

7. Finally, as a thumb rule, the dealing in cash should be restricted. There must be a prefixed list of items and transactions that can be transacted in cash and that cannot.

Banks

1. Wherever practical, you must have joint signatories on all payments being made from company account and a proper chain of approval should be maintained in writing.

2. All the checkbooks should be kept in a safe box and should be under the accountability of most senior resources in accounts and under no circumstances the signing of blank cheques should be an allowed activity.

3. All the cancelled cheques must be defaced and maintained by the Accounts Department until a certain time or the completion of a statutory audit. The bank must be reconciled either on a daily or weekly basis looking at the number of transactions and practicality.

4. For all the bank balances, you must talk to your banker to maintain these balances in a money multiplier or a two-in-one system wherein your balance could earn some interest and your liquidity is not challenged. If this facility is not available, then you may go for OD against the FD at least for surplus funds.

5. As a matter of internal check and control, the person authorizing the invoice and making the payment should be two different individuals, if possible.

HR matters

1. There should be a system for the issuance of offer letters and appointment letters and maintenance of employee files. This, among other basic documents related to employees, should contain necessary company communication like confirmation, warning and appreciation.

2. There should be an employee muster roll system in place. The processing of salaries should be linked to the attendance system of the company. Two different individuals should do attendance management and salary processing.

3. The company must follow a grade and scale system for the payment of salaries and other benefits. This helps in new hiring as well as maintaining the synergy among the employees of various departments and results in a balanced work culture.

4. There must be properly drafted reward and recognition plans and proper communication of the same to all employees. The sweat equity and ESOP plan should also be disclosed and discussed as and when applicable.

5. The company must maintain proper retention strategies and a dynamic training calendar for its employees.

Sales and debtors (receivables)

1. The company must have a formal accounts receivable policy mentioning the invoice schedules, checkpoints of sale and amount of invoice. So, the "when", "what" and "how" of the invoicing must be crystal clear to the accounts receivable team.

2. A robust credit policy saves the company from becoming a forced lender and thus reducing the working capital. The accounts receivables team must know the credit history and credit limit of the

invoiced customer and due dates for collection. Collection timeliness and credit rating go hand in hand.

3. The commencement of work/service and delivery of goods and dispatch thereof should not begin without receipt and recording of a valid purchase order of the buyer or client. The PO formats and terms and conditions must also be noticed and analyzed.

4. The invoicing process should be made automated and, if possible electronic with the capacity to generate the outstanding report, overdue report, receivables ageing and exception report. These reports become the input for deciding the internal rating and creditworthiness of the client. The client credit limit must be reviewed in line with payment history as frequently as possible and practical.

5. A robust and time bound collection process and standard collection system are crucial. It should indicate the steps to be taken while collecting, starting from humble reminder calls, negotiation, letter of request, legal letter and litigation. The steps like cash discount too could be afforded in an appropriate situation to enhance the collection quality. Also, all collections must be allocated to the right invoice than just crediting the client account.

Purchases and creditors (payables)

1. The company must have accounts payable policy that defines the purchase process clearly along with the well-defined roles and monetary limits of the team. Authority matrix for both revenue and capital purchases at various levels of hierarchy is a must phenomenon.

2. There must be an appropriate process for on-boarding the vendors and suppliers wherein the quality and price, etc. could be kept in check. Empanelment and blacklisting of vendors should be done in a defined way. The employee's related parties should be closely

monitored by taking the declaration and indemnities. There are multiple databases available for blacklisted businesses and the same should be kept in mind while signing off the order.

3. Unless there is already a standard empanelled supplier who is best suited to the company, there should be three quotes system and the lowest price offer with maintained quality level should be accepted.

4. Before any accounts payable invoice is paid, there must be a three-way check that includes the valid purchase order, a valid goods inward movement receipt (gate receipt) and the final invoice describing the earlier two. The person who is receiving the goods/service should be delinked to the invoice verification process.

5. The incidences of errant purchase orders, partly completed KYC and on-boarding compliance, early or late payment than due dates and any uneven practice of discounts must be deeply analyzed for the early detection of any internal or external fraud.

Inventory/stocks

1. Depending on the size of the company, a good inventory management system that follows the simple in and out balances is a must for any kind of stock. The system should be able to generate the physical count record at any point in time.

2. As frequently as possible, the physical count of inventory is a must activity and analyzing the causes of difference if any is even more important.

3. The stocks should be classified basis value, usage frequency and type in such a way that the most valued are most safe and the frequently used ones are at most easy places to save man-hours for handling those.

4. The optimum quantity of stock must be analyzed quantitatively as well as qualitatively to help the company reduce its working capital

deployment and hence support the higher profit. Depending upon the size of the order and other relevant factors, the mechanism of "on-demand supply of material" can be a good practice to save the freight cost of raw material if such arrangements are utilized optimally.

The above internal control and checkpoints are not exhaustive and are important for maintaining basic hygiene. In the absence of any regular internal audit team, you may implement and monitor these checkpoints with the help of one or more staff that has the auditing skill sets and the right temperament. However, you must seek the help of a professional internal auditor on a regular basis. The ideal frequency shall be monthly however, if there is a budget constraint, then quarterly. You must not get confused between the benefits of internal audit and annual company audits.

Risk Analysis and Management

Risk is something that is inherent in every business decision, be it macro-level risks like global, country, industry or micro-level risks like a specific company or project risk. So, the first categorization of risks basis their source of origin are as follows:

a. **Global economy risk:** This includes a specific risk from a foreign country and foreign exchange related exposures Covid 19 pandemic is a good example of global economy risk.

b. **Macroeconomic or national-level risk:** GDP/NNP or political risk like minority government, etc.

c. **Industry risk:** There could be technological or legal changes that may affect the business. There could also be unethical competition risk in a particular industry.

d. **The firm risk or corporate risk:** There could be risks like promoter background and collection cycle and the type of target customer.

e. **Project risk:** There could be a risk pertaining to the fact that the cost of the fund might be higher than the expected return on the project. This could be an estimation error or timing error. This could be analyzed as standalone or in the context of prevailing market conditions.

We analyze the project risk through different techniques depending upon our precise goal. The techniques like breakeven, sensitivity, scenario, simulation and decision tree are best for doing standalone risk profiling for a project.

The project risk analysis on a standalone basis is a little easier as compared to contextual corporate risk. The corporate risk is complex to analyze and equally technical to mitigate because it runs on many pillars that are not under our direct control.

All these project risks put together on a standalone basis along with capital structure decisions (including the overall capital infusion and commencement of business) when seen in one single parlance are known as the total business risk or overall corporate risk.

The corporate risk can be further uncluttered into five different buckets and which are follows:

a. Financial risk

b. Technological risk

c. Performance risk

d. Economic risk

e. Regulatory risk

These overall business risks are always seen together. For example, if a business has a high ROI but does not have skilled manpower in the operating geography, the performance risk becomes absolute and you just cannot remove or mitigate it.

No business is absolutely free of risks in its journey of growth and stability, specifically in its early stages. Both an early start-up and an established business face different levels and types of risks. While the former fears the risk of survival, the latter fears the risk of sustainability and perpetuity. The business has to navigate carefully through these uneven internal as well as external situations to grow out from these constant clouds of existence risk.

For managing the different categories of risks, business owners always align their strategies to mitigate these risks. Just like the example mentioned above wherein a business with good ROI faces performance risk, owners might decide to establish the operating office and the corporate headquarter in two different geographies. This, as a result, might mitigate the risk if not remove the same totally.

The basic steps towards managing these business risks always start with proper identification and then analyzing it carefully through a few scenario analysis or other similar tools. Once the analysis is done, the next step shall be to understand the severity of risk both in terms of absolute damages and its controllability. If this risk is manageable or controllable then the cost-benefit analysis should be done. The success of risk management depends upon the severity and timing of such risk and then constant monitoring of the circumstantial events and finally a timely and impactful action.

There could be short-term and long-term risks too. Short-term risks are not enduring in nature, and you can keep avoiding those while keeping the focus on priorities.

On the other hand, long-term risk affects business in the long run. Therefore, a more detailed analysis should be done and a mitigation plan should be enforced. These plans of mitigation and management of risk are technically called Enterprise Risk Management (ERM). While making an ERM, the following guidelines need to be kept in mind:

1. Align your risk with your long-term strategies in such a way that the timing of funding and initiation of the capital plan could correlate and you do not get into unnecessary leverage.

2. Document the risk management and mitigation policy properly, and these should explain the roles of the board, management and staff clearly in the hour of need.

3. For unforeseen and unsystematic risks, adhere to insurance policies and business hedging instruments that are commonly used in the market to ward off a few uncertainties. Always consider business insurance and hedging cost into your operating budget.

4. Adopt a flexible approach while planning for risk management. A matrix of authorities and business priorities should be planned proactively and ideally before any risk hits you.

5. Your bank balance and treasury function should not be compromised and the treasury should have no or least responsibilities to make up the business operating loss. At times, the business owners put their idle capital into speculation and risky stocks that expose the business to a different kind of uncontrollable risk.

6. Build some safety margins while planning for capital expenditure. So, plan the expenses upward and revenue downwards. This is the simple principle of conservatism that helps keep your business, within yardsticks of measurement by any third party.

7. The overall business plan must have a few versions that explain various scenarios and output sensitivity towards change in key factors of a business.

8. Creating a risk management program that is forward-looking is a key goal for management. Rather than keeping stagnant programs that require an overhaul to change, companies can

keep building up such risk management measures and refine performance with proper planning and implementation of the ERM. So, the ERM program should be dynamic, agile and non-static.

The scope of ERM is much broader than just protecting physical and financial assets. With an ERM approach, the scope of risk management is enterprise-wide, and the application of risk management is targeted to enhancing and protecting the unique combination of tangible and intangible assets comprising the organization's business model, with an equal focus on the earning capacity of these underlying business assets.

Chapter 3.10

Prediction of Sickness and Recovery

Just like humans are prone to sickness so are businesses, and we should accept it as a normal occurrence and treat it through the adoption of internal discipline (like change in lifestyle) or external stimulus (like drugs or surgery).

The sickness could be defined in terms of the net worth as well as cash flow. The Reserve Bank of India (RBI), defines a sick unit as "one which has incurred cash losses in one year and, in the judgment of financing bank, is likely to incur cash loss for the current year as well as the following year and/or there is an imbalance in  the business's financial structure, that is current ratio is less than 1:1 and the debt-equity ratio is worsening." In the case of micro and small enterprises, it is defined as a unit with a borrowing account that remains NPA for a period of at least three months or the accumulated losses become 50% of the net worth.

So, business sickness is a macro situation wherein an adverse situation makes the perpetuity of the business unviable and the business is predicted to be not able to meet its obligation as and when they arise.

The sickness may be caused by two macro factors:

a. Internal factor

b. External factors

The **internal factors** primarily refer to the deficiency in management and running of a business, and it may include the followings:

1. Ineffective and incompetent leadership

2. Inadequate and unskilled manpower resources

3. Wrong capital structure

4. Poor financial management

5. Improper marketing and sales strategy like pricing methods and poor branding

6. A poor quality-control mechanism

7. Inadequate infrastructure or technical non-viability

8. Inappropriate location

9. Bad investor management

The **external factors** refer to all those prevailing circumstances, events and occurrences that happen outside the business but have a significant adverse impact on business operations. External factors are as follows:

1. Natural calamities having a direct adverse effect

2. Macro change in the national economy

3. Macro change in the global economy

4. A sudden shift in the preference of consumers in the favour of competitors

5. The cancellation of major purchase/sales orders beyond the control of the business

6. The invention and development of new technology or products

7. A change in credit policies and banking outlook towards a business segment

It is possible that the occurrence of such factors or events may or may not affect the business. In such cases, it is important to know the symptoms of the business sickness, which can be seen through the following indicators:

a. Irregular banking transactions

b. Dishonour of cheques and other instalments of repayments

c. Untimely and delayed payment to suppliers

d. Excessive employee turnover

e. Poor maintenance of the office and plant

f. Frequent need for loans, overdraft and borrowings

g. Accumulation of inventory of either finished good or raw materials

h. Suppliers changing their credit terms and asking for more and more advances with purchase orders

i. Non-payments of government taxes and delayed filing of periodical returns of sale or income

j. Inability to take trade discounts from the market and getting funds at the standard market rate

While it is important to know the causes and symptoms, it is equally important to know the solution, which can be categorized into three stages.

- Predicting the sickness
- Stages of sickness
- Solution and steps to recover from sickness

Though the prediction can be done subjectively looking at the financial ratios and comparing them with the industry norms and historical data of the company, there have been various types of research wherein the multiple ratios of business are read together and interpreted. When we use company data and ratio and compare the same with other businesses in the same industry, we call that univariate analysis. When the multiple ratios and relationship between various variables are read together and then compared with a fixed industry index, we call that multivariate analysis.

Depending upon the stage of business sickness, we apply the appropriate treatment and identify the problem (severity of sickness), which is the first step towards solving the same. One can categorize the sickness level of business on various scales but renowned management Guru Jim Collins has beautifully defined the stages of sickness in his book named 'How the Mighty Falls'. According to him, the following could be defining stages:

1. Hubris

Stage 1 kicks in when people become arrogant regarding success, virtually as an entitlement, and they lose sight of the true underlying factors that created success in the first place.

2. Undisciplined pursuit of more

Companies in Stage 2 stray from the disciplined creativity that led them to greatness in the first place, making undisciplined leaps into areas where they cannot be better.

3. Denial of risk

At this stage, leaders discount negative data, amplify positive data and put a positive spin on ambiguous data. They simply ignore the existing internal risk in the garb of external factors or consider those as "temporary" or "cyclic" and continue to believe that their fundamentals are strong.

4. Grasping for salvation

The cumulative baggage and risk of the previous stages, assert themselves throwing the enterprise into a sharp decline. The leadership responds by taking bold decisions such as acquisition or hiring of a CEO in place of getting back to the disciplines that brought success in the first place. Initial results from taking dramatic action may appear positive, but they do not last long.

5. Irrelevance or death

The longer a company remains in Stage 4, repeatedly grasping for silver bullets, the more likely it will fall in the trap. At this stage, accumulated setbacks erode the financial strength and individual spirit to such an extent that leaders sell out the business, and in extreme cases, the enterprise simply dies its own death.

For the revival of the sick business unit, the viability study should be done to assess whether the business can be revived or not. The viability study must encompass a comprehensive assessment in all areas of operations starting from finance and HR to market and competition.

Once the viability is assessed and the business is found to be revivable, revival plans are made and appropriate actions are taken, which, among others, may include the followings:

1. Settlement with banks
2. Settlement with creditors
3. Divestment and disposal of non-viable units/assets
4. A remake of business strategy and marketing plan

5. Employee ownership and participation

6. Change of management

7. Provision of additional finance

8. Cost cuttings in operations and capital

9. Debt restructuring and waiver of interest or penalty

10. Conversion of third-party liabilities into equity

There could be a situation where the cost of revival is more than the benefits of revival and in that case, it is better to let it go. There are many options available to such companies for winding up and one of them these days is application to appropriate authorities for the commencement of corporate insolvency and resolution proceedings under the Insolvency and Bankruptcy Code of India.

The morale remains that "prevention is better than cure" and so one should apply all intelligence to observe the early symptoms and stages of sickness and take immediate remedial action to avoid the painful end.

Restructuring, Merger and Acquisition

Corporate restructuring is the process of redesigning one or more aspects of a company and this may include any change in a company's capital structure, operations flow and mechanics, selling any  business unit or assets class or acquiring ownership of any business unit. The process of reorganizing a company may be implemented due to a number of reasons starting from productivity enhancement and cost reduction to a financial restructuring like mergers, acquisitions, takeover, demerger, divestitures or alliances.

Corporate structuring happens mainly for the following reasons:

A. **Change in the strategic priorities:** The company attempts to improve its performance by eliminating certain business units that do not align with the core focus of the company and do not seem to fit strategically with the long-term vision of the company.

B. **Lack of profit:** The division may not be profitable enough to cover the firm's cost of capital, and therefore cause economic losses to the firm.

C. **Cash flow requirement:** The sale of a division can help in creating a considerable cash inflow for the company, which, in turn, can be put to use for generating better returns.

D. **Complementary resources:** If two companies have complementary resources that augment each other, then the combined value shall be better for shareholders. This strategy also cuts the cost of back-end management and so becomes an effective reason for merger decisions.

E. **Utilization of surplus fund:** Sometimes a mature business generates surplus cash reserves over a period of time. In such cases, rather than distributing the dividend, the idea of acquiring a new business can further increase the profit for shareholders.

F. **Reverse synergy:** According to reverse synergy, the individual parts may be worth more than the combined unit. This is the common reason for divesting the assets.

G. **Industry consolidation:** Consolidation of the industry is an important driver for business acquisition and mergers around the globe.

H. **Competition management and tax planning perspective** could also trigger business reconstruction decisions, but those cases are few.

Originating from the cause of such a decision, restructuring transactions may be broadly classified into two categories.

A. **Acquisition:** Here, the businesses are either merged, amalgamated or bought out or taken over. Essentially, in these transactions, one business buys into another. Examples are merger, buy-out, takeover, leveraged buy-out and business alliances.

B. **Divestitures:** While acquisition decision refers to buying an asset or business and getting control of the company, the divestiture results in contraction of assets and control. Examples are partial sell-off, sale of equity stake, demerger, equity carve-out, etc.

A merger takes place when two companies combine together as equals to form an entirely new company, which is a rare scenario. Since mostly one company acquires another company the process is more of absorption of operations of the target company. But for sake of morale comfort to employees and owners of the acquired entity, we still use the word merger instead of acquisition. On the basis of the nature of the acquisition, the merger may be broadly categorized into the following segments:

a. Horizontal merger

A horizontal merger is a merger of nearly equal-sized companies that operate in the same line of business or industry. Companies, in this case, are usually direct competitors, and these mergers are more of industry consolidation. Example: if Hindustan Lever acquires Colgate Palmolive.

b. Vertical merger

When two companies, which are in the value chain of producing the same good and services at a different stage of production, decide to merge, it is called a vertical merger. For example, a clothing store takes over a yarn manufacturing unit.

c. Concentric merger

When a merger happens between firms that serve the same customer-base in a particular industry but offer different products and services, it is called concentric mergers. Their products may complement each other, but they are technically not the same products. For example, a computer hardware company acquires a software company.

d. Conglomerate merger

The merger between two companies that operate in a completely different industry and are at different stages of production and have different sizes is known as a conglomerate merger. This is usually done to diversify into other business lines to reduce risks and enhance profits.

Mergers and acquisitions (M&A) are complicated legal and financial processes that rely on deep financial analysis and terms and conditions that have future implications. Below is a list of best practices in chronological order (approximately) for the acquiring/buying company:

- Understand the target company's position before initiating contact and be sensitive to how it might receive your offer. Use absolute diplomacy

- Employ and retain experienced leadership/advisors/investment bankers

- Keep culture convergence in mind. One of the acquisitions in these transactions is talent pool too, and so the same should be preserved at all cost unless the synergetic demand is something else.

- Develop trust and transparency between the lead consultant, investment bankers and seller. Keep communication open among all parties throughout the process.

- Create a time-bound post-acquisition plan so that you do not head into integration blindly. This is more needed when you are going for a strategic investment.

- Monitor the success of the investment decision and synergy value till complete integration of culture and operation.

For the target/selling company:

- Do not get excited at the first offer. Know the strength of your position and involve independent valuers of repute

- Employ and retain experienced financial and legal advisors who will have your best interests in mind

- Understand the valuation perspective and plan for better valuation by showcasing higher profits through cost control, etc.

- Analyze multiple offers to increase the valuation

- Sign the non-conflict and non-compete clauses in legal agreements carefully including the applicable period of such clauses

Throughout the process, issues are bound to arise on both the buyer's and seller's sides. Both parties should resist the urge to get too emotional or latch onto extreme measures.

Typically, in a merger transaction, the acquiring company may compensate either in stocks or cash and what is most important here is the exchange ratio. For being doubly sure on such ratio that defines the compensation quantum, go for market-related standalone multiple for any consummated deal in the past and compare the same with an underlying valuation of subject companies.

In India, mergers and acquisitions are governed and regulated by the Companies Act 2013, SEBI Act, and Competition Act. The Companies Act is there for taking care of creditors' interest, SEBI for shareholders and the Competition Commission for

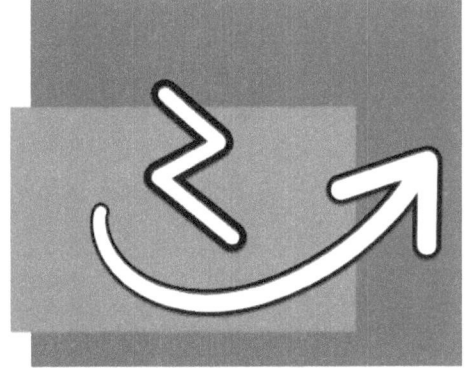

restricting the unfair trade practices that encourage the growth of the monopoly of a few companies. For any merger in India, one needs to pass through the approval process of the Companies Act through the designated court/NCLT (national company law tribunals).

As these decisions are big in terms of money and the exit cost is prohibitory, therefore, a company must focus on all possible dimensions and detailing to estimate the synergic value accurately along with controlled and time-bound post-acquisition integration process for creating real value through these restructuring decisions.

SME Initial Public Offering (IPO)

Rather than taking money from an institution or group of wealthy people, when you offer the ownership units (shares of the company) to the public at large, the process is known as an initial public offering (IPO). It is an interesting fact that the famous Dutch East India Company was the first company to issue bonds and stocks.

Governments and economists all over the world have realized the importance of the SME sector as drivers of the economic development of the country. The biggest key factor impeding the growth and sustenance of these SMEs is their access to capital and terms attached to raising such capital.

To overcome this, almost all developed nations and capital markets have realized the need for a separate exchange for the SME segment wherein some leniency with the level of financial performance and compliance could be accepted for the companies of a certain size.

In India, the framework for setting up SME exchanges was conceptualized by SEBI in 2008 and after four years of brainstorming sessions at various authorities, the BSE SME and NSE Emerge platforms were established as SME wings of our main board exchange BSE and NSE.

The BSE and the NSE have strict eligibility criteria that must be adhered to in order to list company shares on their platforms. On the other hand, the BSE SME and NSE Emerge platform's eligibility criteria are not so strict and allow flexibility in terms of capital size, underwriting, pricing or application values. Listing of shares on these small company exchanges proves to be a stepping stone for listing the shares at the main board in due course of time.

SME listing not only provides financial benefits and leverage but also benefits its investors as it provides an exit route to private equity investors.

Qualifying the listing requirements for any stock exchange indicates good governance and efficient trade practices, and as a result, this raises the company's credentials with customers, partners, suppliers, investors, banks and the media. This in turn helps guarantee continued financial support and liquidity in the company.

Though there could be few process differences, depending upon the stock exchange, the following is an overview of the process and activities of an IPO:

1. Selecting merchant banker
2. Restructuring capital and valuation
3. Appointing bankers, registrars, market makers, etc.
4. Checking due diligence and compliance for IPO

5. Preparing, filing and approving offer documents with the stock exchange and ROC

6. Conducting a marketing strategy research and effective corporate communication based on the strength of the company

7. Opening, closing and allocating equity

8. Listing and trading at the exchange

Even though there are a number of common listing requirements, there could be few differences in the eligibility of BSE SME and NSE EMERGE platform. Therefore, I am categorizing both separately. Though the information given hereunder are updated but you are suggested to check the latest requirement or process change, as on date of your IPO decision.

S. No.	Particulars of requirement	BSE SME	NSE EMERGE
1.	Organization structure	Public company	Any company
2.	Company's net worth	Rs. 3 crores of net worth	Not required
3.	Minimum net tangible assets	Rs. 3 crores	Not required

4.	Profitability track record	2 out of the last 3 years in profit	2 out of the last 3 years in profit
5.	Minimum post paid-up capital	Rs. 3 crores	No minimum
6.	Maximum paid-up capital	Rs. 25 crores	Rs. 25 crores
7.	Audited finances/ annual returns of last 3 to 5 years	Required	Required
8.	The company should not have any admitted winding-up petition	Required	Required
9.	Minimum number of allottees at the time of listing	50	50
10.	Auditor certificate of no default to any bank or financial institution	Required	Required
11.	DEMATED shares	Required	Required
12.	Underwriting of Issue	100% (15% by merchant banker)	100% (15% by merchant banker)

13.	No reference to BIFR (Board for Industrial and financial reconstruction) ever	Required	Required
14.	Corporate website with a code of conduct	Required	Required
15.	Minimum application amount or trading lot size	Rs. 1 lakh	Rs. 1 lakh
16.	Minimum public shareholding	25%	25%
17.	Market maker	Registered with exchange	Registered with exchange
18.	Promoter or associated enterprises details of any civil/criminal/legal cases to be disclosed	Required	Required

Once the eligibility is established and the company decides to go for an IPO, it has to follow certain steps in order to save time. It is better and necessary to commence some of the processes simultaneously rather than waiting for the previous one to finish. The process flow chart for SME IPO is as follows:

```
┌─────────────────────────────────────────────────────────────────┐
│ Conversion of business entity into LLC/Public Company as per the  │
│ Companies Act 2013                                                │
└─────────────────────────────────────────────────────────────────┘
                                  ↓
┌─────────────────────────────────────────────────────────────────┐
│ Appointment of financial, legal and secretarial consultant and    │
│ merchant banker                                                   │
└─────────────────────────────────────────────────────────────────┘
                                  ↓
┌─────────────────────────────────────────────────────────────────┐
│ Identification and appointment of a registrar, transfer agent and │
│ market maker                                                      │
└─────────────────────────────────────────────────────────────────┘
                                  ↓
┌─────────────────────────────────────────────────────────────────┐
│ Submission of master form with NSDL, CSDL, signing of agreement   │
│ and receipt of ISIN                                               │
└─────────────────────────────────────────────────────────────────┘
                                  ↓
┌─────────────────────────────────────────────────────────────────┐
│ Corporate website, hosting of the code of conduct and formation   │
│ of necessary committees like investor grievances, etc.            │
└─────────────────────────────────────────────────────────────────┘
                                  ↓
┌─────────────────────────────────────────────────────────────────┐
│ Identification of peer review auditors and getting the requisite  │
│ audit done                                                        │
└─────────────────────────────────────────────────────────────────┘
                                  ↓
┌─────────────────────────────────────────────────────────────────┐
│ Preparing and filing project report and offer document/ DRHP with │
│ stock exchange                                                    │
└─────────────────────────────────────────────────────────────────┘
                                  ↓
┌─────────────────────────────────────────────────────────────────┐
│ Filing of Prospectus (DRHP) with ROC after in-principal approval  │
│ from stock exchange                                               │
└─────────────────────────────────────────────────────────────────┘
                                  ↓
┌─────────────────────────────────────────────────────────────────┐
│ Filing of final prospectus with SEBI and stock exchange           │
└─────────────────────────────────────────────────────────────────┘
                                  ↓
┌─────────────────────────────────────────────────────────────────┐
│ Opening of issue and closure as per the timeline pre-decided and  │
│ approved earlier                                                  │
└─────────────────────────────────────────────────────────────────┘
                                  ↓
┌─────────────────────────────────────────────────────────────────┐
│ Coordination among banker, RTA and issuer and filing of basis of  │
│ allocation to stock exchange and Demat credit of shares           │
└─────────────────────────────────────────────────────────────────┘
                                  ↓
┌─────────────────────────────────────────────────────────────────┐
│ Filing of listing application with stock exchange for listing and │
│ trading permission                                                │
└─────────────────────────────────────────────────────────────────┘
                                  ↓
┌─────────────────────────────────────────────────────────────────┐
│ Issue newspapers advertisement within 10 days of completion of    │
│ IPO and grant of trading licenses from exchange                   │
└─────────────────────────────────────────────────────────────────┘
```

Many promoters have a feeling of loss of control and fear of hostile takeover, but in view of robust regulations to curb the hostile takeover, these situations are ruled out. One must appreciate that as now the money from the public is involved, better internal control and stricter compliances shall be enforced and that is better even for benchmarking with a peer group of companies. Over and above, the strict compliance of securities laws, the finance and secretarial departments must be geared for quarterly governance report and shareholder accounts report along with six-monthly financial reports.

For the SME companies to migrate to the main board, the steps are very simple as compared to the one who goes for listing directly on the main board. Once an SME completes two years at the SME exchange and has paid-up capital of more than Rs. 10 crores, it can apply for the main board listing, which is subject to other procedural requirements.

.

Financial Glossary

- **Account:** A record of expenses, assets, liabilities and income kept by a company, bank or any other entity.

- **Accounting date:** The last date of the period covered by an organization's annual accounts.

- **Actuary:** An expert on long-term funds, retirement scheme, assets and debts, life expectancy and risk for insurance purposes

- **Acquisition:** The buying of one company by another. It may be friendly or hostile.

- **Annual cover:** An insurance policy to cover the exigencies that a person/business must renew every year, such as health or car insurance

- **Annual report:** A report issued by the company every year to its shareholders containing the audited financials, director's report and future plans.

- **After-tax:** An amount of money that is left after the payment of required taxes.

- **Amortization:** A process of repayment of a certain loan over a period of time or charging of expenditure in more than one financial period.

- **Annual service:** A check made once a year on business or piece of equipment to make sure that it is working properly

- **Arbitrage:** A combination of sale and purchase in different time or geography to derive benefit from the price difference

- **Arrears:** An overdue amount that was due but not paid

- **Articles of association:** A company's document that sets out the shareholders' rights and the directors' powers and other terms of running a company

- **Audit:** An independent examination of an organization's records and accounts to make sure that they show a fair and accurate view of the financial position of the company at the accounting date

- **Auditor's report:** A report by an independent auditor on an organization's financial records and statements

- **Authorized share capital:** The highest amount of share capital that a company can issue, as set out by the company's memorandum of association

- **Balance brought forward:** An amount shown on a person's last statement that is brought forward to the next statement either to show money saved or money owed

- **Balance sheet:** A summary of a company's assets (what a company owns) and liabilities (debts a company owes) at a point in time

- **Bankruptcy order:** An order issued by the court when a person cannot repay their debts, which allows the person's property to be sold to raise money to pay their creditors

- **Barter:** A way of paying for things by exchanging goods and services instead of money

- **Book value:** The value of a fixed asset, such as a building or machine, after depreciation, as recorded in an organization's accounts. Basically, the real net worth of an item which may be an asset or the company overall.

- **Books of account:** Books that a business must keep to record its financial transactions accurately and fairly

- **Break-even:** A point at which a company earns as much money as it is spending with no profit or loss.

- **Bridging loan:** A loan given by a lending institution to bridge the time difference between outflow and inflow

- **Budget:** A plan of income and expenses during a time period

- **Budget deficit:** A gap that occurs when one plans to spend more money than it earns

- **Capital expenditure:** Money a business spends on buying or improving its fixed assets, such as equipment or furniture

- **Capital gain:** Money a business or person makes if it sells a long-term asset, such as a building, for more than its effective cost

- **Cash inflow:** The amount of money coming into a business

- **Cash outflow:** The amount of money paid in a business

- **Cash flow:** A record of all the money coming in minus all the payments as they are made, measured for a particular time period

- **Collateral:** An asset offered to or needed by a lender as security for a loan, such as a house for a mortgage or factory/plant for an overdraft facility

- **Consumer:** A person who buys a good or service

- **Counterfeit:** Something that a person forges or copies with the aim of deceiving another person

- **Contract of service:** A contract usually agreed between an employee and their employer. A command is given here to do something in a defined way

- **Contract for service:** A contract usually agreed between an organization and another organization or a self-employed person, such as a consultant or a contractor. Work is given for completion here.

- **Creditor:** A person or company who is owed money. Company's suppliers basically. Also known as accounts payable.

- **Creditor turnover:** Average days of payment of suppliers or creditors. Also known as accounts payable period/turnover

- **Credit history:** A history of how well a person has been able to repay the debt. Poor credit history means lower chances to get loans.

- **Credit limit:** The highest amount a financing company will lend a person at any time

- **Credit risk:** The risk that a person might not repay a loan or credit

- **Critical illness insurance:** Insurance that pays a lump sum, covers a person's liabilities or makes regular payments if a person cannot work due to a serious illness

- **Current account:** A bank account that lets a person keep their money secure, but still write cheques as and when needed without a debit or credit transaction limit. Basically, a business account.

- **Current assets:** Short-term assets, such as bank balances and stocks that can convert into cash in a short time

- **Current liabilities:** Short-term debts that a business must pay within a year, such as bank overdrafts, money owed to suppliers and employees

- **Debtor:** A person who owes money. Generally, clients and customers. Also known as accounts receivable.

- **Debtor turnover:** Average days of realization of credit sale. Also known as average collection time or collection turnover.

- **Deferred revenue expenditure:** An expenditure which is not a capital expenditure but the benefit is derived over more than one accounting period. For example, a license fee paid for three years.

- **Depreciation:** This is a charge for the use of assets in a particular financial period. This amount is charged to the income statement.

- **Disposable income:** Income available after a person pays tax, loans and buys basic goods and services

- **Dissolve/liquidate:** Formally breaking up or closing down an organization or institution

- **Exchange rate:** A changing rate at which a person can change one country's currency for another's. For example, Rs. 73 for $1

- **Financial lease:** A long-term fully amortized non-cancellable lease. Generally used for the financing of assets.

- **Financial statement:** A company's statement that includes the annual accounts, directors' report and so on as required by the law of the land

- **Financial year:** The year covered by a set of annual financial statements.

- **Financial adviser:** Somebody who studies a company's earnings and spending and advises on how to manage or grow their money

- **Floating charge:** A security created by the company over its changing assets, such as stock and unpaid sums from debtors, in return for a loan; if the company does not make the repayments when they are due, the assets are sold to pay it.

- **Goodwill:** An intangible business asset based on a company's reputation and confidence of repeat customers and connections

- **Gross profit:** Total profit made from selling goods and services after deducting the cost of production

- **Guarantor:** A person who agrees to pay the loan if the person who received the loan, fails to pay

- **Health insurance:** A form of insurance that pays for medical expenses

- **Income:** Money coming in such as sales and revenue from other sources

- **Income tax:** A tax on personal or business income

- **Indemnify:** Protects or insures somebody against being sued for their actions

- **Intangible assets:** Assets that cannot be touched or non-physical, such as goodwill and patent rights

- **Inflation:** An increase in the prices of goods and services, which decreases the purchasing power of money

- **Interest rate:** The percentage that a person receives on their savings or pays on their loan

- **Issued share capital:** Shares that a company has allotted to its shareholders

- **LIBOR:** London Interbank Offering Rate

- **Limited liability:** A statement of the maximum amount a company's shareholders would have to pay if the company gets dissolved

- **Liquidity:** The ability to convert an asset to cash easily and quickly with little or no loss of value

- **Market capitalization:** The value of a company when the number of its issued ordinary shares is multiplied by its market price

- **Memorandum of Association:** A document containing details of a company's name, purposes, share capital and other details

- **MIBOR:** Mumbai Interbank Offering Rate

- **Mortgage:** A loan to buy property/assets. If it is not paid back, the lending agency can take over the property.

- **Negotiable instrument:** A document that a person signs to instruct to pay money to another person or organization

- **Net profit:** The amount of money belonging to a company after deducting operating costs such as salaries, rent and electricity bills

- **Non-profit making Organization (NPO):** An organization, usually a charity or public sector agency, that is formed for the public benefit and not making profits

- **Operating lease:** A short-term cancellable lease wherein the part of assets are given out for use and not fully amortized

- **Overdraft:** A facility from a bank that lets a person access more money than they have in their account against payment of interest

- **Paid-up share capital:** The money that shareholders have paid for the shares issued to them

- **Prospectus:** A document from a company that wishes to sell shares to the public at large, giving details of the company's past performance and its plans for the future

- **Recession:** A major fall in economic activity in a country, such as investing, creating jobs or buying goods and services, over an extended period of time. Also known as the economic slowdown

- **Reserves or free reserves:** Amounts that a company sets aside in yearly profits, which can be spent or invested in later years

- **Retained profits:** Profit earned by a business that has not yet been spent or paid as dividends

- **Rights issue:** An issue of extra shares to a company's shareholders at a discount, based on the number of shares they already hold. Shareholders can sell the rights if they do not wish to use them.

- **Secured loan:** A loan that is borrowed against a particular asset, known as security; if a person cannot make the repayments when they are due, the lender can take ownership of the asset.

- **Share certificate:** A document that certifies who owns shares in a company by indicating the type, amount and serial numbers of shares owned by the shareholder

- **Share price:** The cost of buying a share on the stock market or on an invitation to subscribe.

- **Signatory:** A person who signs a document, such as an application form or cheques

- **Solvency:** The ability to pay debts and obligations from available resources

- **Stamp duty:** A tax levied by the government on a change of ownership of assets/shares/rights

- **Statutory accounts:** Company accounts that must be made by the company as per companies act and other applicable laws of the land

- **Statutory audit:** An audit, required by law, of a company's accounts by qualified accountants.

- **Tax credit:** The amount of income tax, which has already been deducted by the payer and for which credit is given when calculating the tax liability of the payee.

- **Tax evasion:** An illegal way of reducing the amount of tax a person owes, for example by concealing income or forging expenses.

- **Tax return:** A form that a person/company must file with revenue authority to record their income and any allowances for the year

- **Term loan:** A loan that a person or organization must repay within a certain period

- **Term-end insurance:** A type of insurance wherein a person's life is secured with a big sum for a small amount. Insurance shall pay only if the insured person dies.

- **Travellers' cheques:** Cheques in a certain currency that a person buys and signs before they leave for another country and that they can encash abroad

- **Underwriting:** A guarantee given by a company to subscribe for unsubscribed shares or pay a certain amount on the occurrence of certain events. The underwriter charges the underwriting commission.

- **Unsecured loan:** A loan that is not backed by a particular asset

- **Upfront fee:** A fee that a person owes or must pay in advance for the commencement of a process or work

- **Valuation point:** The date and time when a valuer value the company or assets or liabilities or the equity

- **Variable interest rate:** An interest rate that is likely to go up or down over time depending upon macroeconomic factors like LIBOR. This is also known as the fluctuating interest rate.

- **Working capital:** The amount of money available to a business in the short-term to bridge the gap between payables and receivables. It is the difference between current assets and current liabilities.

- **Written down value:** Balance value of an asset that is left after charging the depreciation for a period of use. This is also a methodology of charging depreciation.

- **Yield:** The money made on an investment each year, expressed as a percentage of investment

- **Zero-base budgeting:** When there is no reference to historical data and a new budget is made for a new period on the minute justification of each item

- **Zero-coupon bond:** A bond issued at a big discount payable in the future at full value. No interest is paid during the maturity period.

Notes

www.ingramcontent.com/pod-product-compliance
Lightning Source LLC
Chambersburg PA
CBHW030612220526
45463CB00004B/1266